Ulysses on Montmartre:

An Earlier Ulysses in Another Nighttown

Ulysses on Montmartre:

An Earlier Ulysses in Another Nighttown

A French shadow play (1910), its translation, and an
essay on its relation to Joyce's *Ulysses*

by

Akram Midani and
Erwin R. Steinberg

Carnegie Mellon University Press
Pittsburgh 2002

Acknowledgments:

For Watfa and Beverly

We owe a debt to:

—Robert Mehrabian and Paul Christiano,
   who supported this work

—Cynthia Lamb, who edited it carefully, and

—Todd Sanders, who designed it artfully

Not for sale in France.

Library of Congress Control Number: 01-086378

ISBN 0-88748-359-3

Contents

Ulysses on Montmartre

An Earlier Ulysses in Another Nighttown   7

Notes to the Essay   29

Bibliography   33

❖ ❖ ❖

Ulysses in Montmartre

Prologue   42
First Tableau   48
Second Tableau   68
Third Tableau   84

Notes to the Text   89

Biographies   99

An Earlier Ulysses in Another Nighttown
Akram Midani
Erwin R. Steinberg

On December 28, 1887, following a brief experimentation with guignols, puppet-theater performances, Montmartre's shadow theater was born in Rodolphe Salis's legendary Chat Noir and quickly spread to other cabarets in that district (Cate, 50, 55, 63). The shadow theater was a major factor in the success of the Chat Noir until that cabaret closed in February of 1897 (Cate, 58-59). But the shadow theater was picked up and continued in a variety of cabarets on Montmartre, especially in Les Quat'z'Arts and La Lune Rousse, in which Dominique Bonnaud, Numa Blès, and to a lesser extent, Lucien Boyer, played important roles. With the closing of La Chaumiere in 1923, shadow theater seems to have come to an end in Montmartre, its popularity probably undermined by the motion picture (Jeanne, 109).

Shadow Plays

Shadow plays, les *ombres Chinoises* to the French, originated in the Far East and became popular in France in the eighteenth century. They were "a form of puppetry in which flat, jointed figures are passed between a translucent screen and lighted candles . . . so that the audience, seated in front, sees only their shadows. . . . [I]n 1774 Dominique Seraphin opened a theater devoted to them in Versailles, moving in 1764 to the Palais Royal." Shadow plays became quite popular toward the end of the nineteenth century not only in Paris, but also in London as the Galanty Show, "usually in Punch and Judy booths with a thin sheet stretched across the opening and candles behind" (Hartnoll, 490).

The popularity of the art form at the end of the nineteenth century sprang from the success of "newly-developed photomechanical relief-printing processes, which easily and inexpensively reproduced high-contrast black and white drawings." Henri Riviere, who initiated and developed the shadow theater, was attracted by the aesthetic possibilities of those new processes and by Japanese color-woodblock prints, "in which silhouettes have a variety of compositional and decorative functions" (Cate, 55):

At first the screen [of the shadow theater] measured almost one meter square. Eventually it was enlarged to 1.12 meters by 1.40 meters with a huge backstage attached to the outside of the building. . . . Essentially, Riviere created a system in which he placed silhouettes of figures, animals, elements of landscape, and so forth, within a wooden framework at three distances from the screen: the closest created an absolutely black silhouette, and the next two created gradations of black to gray, thus suggesting recession into space. [First cardboard and later zinc] silhouettes could be moved across the screen on runners within the frame. Behind the three tiers of silhouettes were sliding structures supporting glass panels, which could be painted in a variety of colors. . . . (Cate, 58-59).

An important artistic trend at the time that shadow theater began was Fumisme, which anticipated Dadaism and Surrealism. According to Georges Fragerolle:

[Fumisme was] to humor what the operetta is to comic opera, satire to caricature, prunes to Hunyadi-Janos water. . . . In order to be considered a wit, sometimes you need only be an ass in a lion's skin; to be a good *fumiste*, it is often necessary to be a lion in the skin of an ass. In the former case the effect is direct; in the latter it is once, twice, often ten times removed (Cate, 23, 89 fn. 19).

The Fumistes and the shadow theater productions, which they influenced, used puns, sexual innuendo, and scatalogical references to shock the bourgeoisie (*Épater la bourgeoisie*) (Cate, 49, 53, 58-59).

We will be interested here, only briefly, in the shadow theater in general, but, more specifically, in a particular shadow play performed (and published) a decade after the turn of the century, perhaps in homage to the earlier period: *Ulysse à Montmartre*. Written by the aforementioned Dominique Bonnaud, Numa Blès, and Lucien Boyer, it was first performed at the Théâtre d'Ombres of Logiz de la Lune Rousse on September 9, 1910. The play is interesting for two reasons:

—as a celebration of the shadow theater a generation earlier and the people who made it flower, the *fumiste* culture of the 1880s and 1890s, and

—as an instantiation of the cultural milieu of the period in which James Joyce began thinking about writing what turned out to be *Ulysses*, with which *Ulysse à Montmartre* shares many interests.

Ulysse à Montmartre

Ulysse à Montmartre was presented at the Théâtre d'Ombres de "La Lune Rousse" on September 9, 1910, and published by the Sociéte d'Editions de "La Lune Rousse" (Paris, n. d.). Its subtitle was "Legende Neo-Grecque, en un Prologue et Trois Tableaux."[1]

Joyce's *Ulysses*, of course, chronicles the peregrinations of a "modern" (but unknowing) Ulysses in contemporary Dublin. In the French play, however, Ulysses himself appears in pre-Christian Montmartre. In the Prologue, "The Narrator" announces that "Montmartre was discovered by the Greeks over three thousand years ago"—discovered, in fact—by "the subtle Ulysses."[2]

In Scene One, Ulysses and his men arrive at the foot of Montmartre in a trireme "around the year 1000 before Jesus Christ," to the considerable interest of the local population. He is taken to the Hotel of the Peloponesis and Reunited Voyagers and then asks a convenient bearded poet about "this country, who are its gods, what are its mores, and who are its principal inhabitants." The poet responds in eighteen stanzas of six lines each: Montmartre is "a hill of pleasure, / It is a hill of love"; women's fashions proclaim their sexuality; singers and minstrels abound; inhabitants ape the fashionable; streetwalkers, courtesans, and their pimps stroll openly. It is an environment that would tempt even those models of rectitude, Plato and Lycurgus: "Plato will become a mere satyr / And Lycurgus a lecherous old man." Ulysses, the poet warns, will have his virtue sorely tried.

In Scene Two, Ulysses and his men are taken to nighttown and delivered into the hands of Pompeia, the madam of a bordello, who presents Ulysses with Anthelmys, "the purest jewel in my chest. . . . There is no man who can resist her."

Ulysses appeals to Athena to protect him, but quickly succumbs to Anthelmys' charms and goes off for a quick wash before partaking. Happily, however, Minerva is watching and takes Anthelmys away "to catch the train to Lesbos," leaving behind an envious Pompeia and a frustrated Ulysses.

In a brief Scene Three, Ulysses and his men leave, "souvenirs" of their stay evident in the rotund bellies of tearful women.

Saluting the Past

One of the most successful of the early shadow plays was *La Tentation de Saint Antoine* (1887) by Henri Rivere (Cate, 58). As our summary of the plot indicates, however, *Ulysse à Montmartre* (1910) could well have been called *La Tentation d'Ulysse*.

Like earlier *fumiste* works, *Ulysse à Montmartre* is designed to shock the bourgeoisie. Anthelmys, brought on to seduce Ulysses, is "the legitimate wife of a rich banker whose house stands in the Agora." So much for middle class virtue! In the play Ulysses sees not only a poet, but women whose breasts overflow their bodices, and "like horses in heat, / Show erection without inhibition," other women with nothing to cover them but a boa, streetwalkers (male and female), and pimps. There are also references to an "umbrella" (slang for condom) and to Montmartre as Mountjoy, "the hill of pleasure . . . the hill of love" (clear references to the *mons veneris*).

In the play, Minerva saves Ulysses by persuading Anthelmys to catch a train to Lesbos, "a dream island of divine happiness, / Where a kiss lingers, / And a caress has no end." This particular stratagem that Minerva uses to save Ulysses would seem to make little sense until one recognizes that at the time Montmartre was also thought of as Mount Lesbos:

Montmartre, the metropolis of anarchists, artists, and all those who, irked by society's laws, elected to despise them, Montmartre, in the 1880s, became the great lesbian centre of Paris. No one there was surprised to see ladies in men's suits, with ties and trilbies, sitting at the café tables. In the Moulin Rouges and the Elysees it was quite acceptable for two women to waltz together, as Lautrec painted them, hatless, in men's jackets and open-necked shirts, clasping one another breast to breast—the best prelude to amorous enjoyment, as Proust's Professor Cottard explained, watching the young girls dancing at the Casino de Balbec (Julian, 88).

Épater la bourgeoisie, indeed!

The *fumistes* also delighted in puns, particularly sexual ones. For example, in 1884 Georges Bézodis "rephrase[d] the main stanza of Aristide Bruant's *Chat noir ballade* . . . to create an obvious lewd pun on the term:

Je cherche fortune, autour du Chat Noir . . . (Bruant)
(I'm seeking fortune, around the Black Cat . . .)

Je cherche ma fortune avec mon Chat Noir . . . (Bezodis)
(I'm seeking my fortune with my black pussy . . .) (Cate, 37)

The authors of our shadow play, similarly, play on the French homophones *salop/salaud* (slut/filthy) and undertake other word plays. *Ulysse à Montmartre*, for example, ends with the claim that Ulysses was "le onzieme arriere-granpére de M. Maurice Donnay, du Chat français et de l'Academie noire" (the eleventh great grandfather of Monsieur Maurice Donnay, of the French Cat and of the Black Academy)—obviously a play on the fact that Donnay was a member of the distinguished French Academy and a poet and author of several shadow plays who had performed at the Chat Noir—the cabaret Black Cat. Our footnotes to the shadow play give many more examples of such word play.[3]

Other Early Plays at Le Chat Noir (1887) and
Their Echoes in *Ulysse à Montmartre* (1910)

Jules Lemaître, in his review (January 3, 1987) of the performance of Caran d'Ache's shadow play *Épopée* at Le Chat Noir, wrote:

[L]ittle silhouettes, cut out in zinc and set moving behind a white cloth little more than a yard in width, could communicate to us a touch of the spirit of war and the sense of grandeur [of the Napoleonic wars from the victory at Austerlitz to the retreat from Russia].

He wrote further that Caran d'Ache,

whose hand is very bold and very sure, contrives to give us an illusion of life from the start by the convincing truth of his simplified little outlines. He has resorted not to caricature but rather to a peculiar method of draughtsmanship which—depicting the faces lying outside its scope—so handles bodies as to intensify their individuality and expressiveness (Lemaître, 307-309).

In his review, Lemaître described *Épopée* as, "in effect, a poem without words and in thirty scenes, the characters in which are *ombres chinoises*" (Lemaître, 307; Segal, 71). In their early stages, French shadow plays impressed largely by their visual inventiveness, but were soon seen "as a distinct art form in themselves" (Segal, 68). They served to bring artists like Caran d'Ache and Henri Riviere to the attention of the public, and these men later went on to become important in the more traditional artistic media. From the first, Salis provided running commentaries, but these seem to have been *ad hoc* improvisations, even, perhaps, *tours de force* in their own right (Segal, 67-69, 70-71). Soon, however, poets and musicians were invited to collaborate with the artists, fulfilling Salis' aspiration for the shadow play to be recognized as a *Gesamtkunstwerke*, or total work of art, which sought a breakdown of traditional barriers between the arts for the sake of their mutual enrichment and the creation of "new" art that would combine the verbal, visual, musical, and choreographic [,] an idea very much in the air at the time (Segal, 20).

Just as *Épopée* was one high point in the history of cabaret theater at Le Chat Noir, *Phryné* was another. It was written by Maurice Donnay, to whom homage is paid, tongue in cheek, at the end of *Ulysse à Montmartre*, 23 years later. Presented at Le Chat Noir on January 9, 1891, and "set in ancient Athens, the work recounts in seven tableaux the trial and eventual acquittal of the voluptuous courtesan Phryné (nicknamed "The Sieve," *le Crible*), who has had the audacity to disrupt at a crucial point the performance of a play about Leda, the wife of King Tynrade, who has grown wary of the love of humans and dreams of the love of the gods." In *Ulysse à Montmartre*, as we have seen, the narrator refers to the story of Leda and the Swan (i.e., Jupiter), which appears as a play within the play *Phryné* (Siegel, 74-75).

Phryné, like the later *Ulysse à Montmartre*, continues the tradition of reinterpreting and reworking the Greek classics, which began in France during the Neo-Classical period. Joyce's *Ulysses*, of course, is also in that tradition. The French play about Ulysses and the Irish novel share a playfulness that is also part of that tradition, for as John Huizinga explains in *Homo Ludens*: "To the degree that belief in the literal truth of the myth diminishes, the play-element, which had been proper to it from the beginning, will re-assert itself with increasing force" (Huizinga, 130).

Ulysse à Montmartre (1910) also paid both real and mock reverence to Donnay's *Phryné* (1891). In its setting it is the obverse of *Phryné*. The earlier play posits a Chat Noir in Athens and for its play-within-a-play (for the story of Leda and the Swan) an Athenian shadow theater (Siegel, 74-75). The later story, instead, brings the Greek Ulysses to France, where the play is put on in the—original—Chat Noir, the Parisian home of the shadow theater. The later play pays homage to the earlier one in its use of a combination of prose and verse and of a *recitant* (narrator or presenter), in references to things that occurred in the earlier play like a reference to the story of Leda and the Swan, in the mention of Phryné as one of "Ces dames" in the second scene, in its authors' choice of an erotic subject, and in its wry tone.

To make the homage clear, there is not only a specific reference to Maurice Donnay, the author of *Phryné*, in the last lines of *Ulysse à Montmartre*, but in those same lines a deliberate (and amusing) reversal of a pair of adjectives, *français* and *noire*: the French text reads *du Chat français et de l'Académie noire* (of the French Cat and of the Black Academy) instead of *du Chat Noir et de l'Académie Française* (of the Black Cat and of the French Academy). Donnay wrote *Phryné* (and also *Ailleurs*, first performed also in 1891) specifically for Le Chat Noir; and he was inducted into the French Academy in 1907 (Siegel, 74-75). Joyce would have appreciated those last lines, the shadow theater equivalent of the good-natured wink and mischievous grin of live actors or dancers that sometimes bring down the curtain in a traditional theater on a piece of whimsy or a spoof.

As we've indicated, an important artistic trend at the time that shadow theater began was Fumisme, which anticipated Dadaism and Surrealism. The Fumistes and the shadow theater productions, which they influenced, used puns, sexual innuendo, and scatalogical references to shock the bourgeoisie (*Épater la bourgeoisie*) (Cate, 49, 53, 58-59). This trend affected not only the early shadow plays on Montmartre, but *Ulysse à Montmartre* as well.

Joyce and Silhouettes

Joyce was not in Paris in the fall of 1910, and we can find no evidence that he saw *Ulysse à Montmartre* later or that he read it, but its authors and Joyce shared some common interests; if Joyce did not see or read it while browsing at Shakespeare and Co., for example, he may well have heard about it.

Whether Joyce was even aware of the shadow theater, in either its French or English forms, he was certainly aware of the principle. Joyce's brother Stanislaus reports that when Joyce was still a "schoolboy," he wrote a series of sketches called *Silhouettes*, probably named after the first of them[4] (although he may also have been influenced by a book of poems of the same title that Arthur Symons published in 1892):

Silhouettes [the first sketch], like the first three stories of *Dubliners*, was written in the first person singular, and described a row of mean little houses along which the narrator passes after nightfall. His attention is attracted by two figures in violent agitation on a lowered window-blind illuminated from within, the burly figure of a man, staggering and threatening with upraised fist, and the smaller sharp-faced figure of a nagging woman. A blow is struck and the light goes out. The narrator waits to see if anything happens afterwards. Yes, the window-blind is illuminated again, dimly, by a candle no doubt, and the woman's sharp profile appears accompanied by two small heads, just above the window-ledge, of children wakened by the noise. The woman's finger is pointed in warning. She is saying, 'Don't waken Pa' (Stanislaus Joyce, 90).

"The Sisters," the first story in Joyce's *Dubliners*, opens with a similar device, although in this instance the "screen" is empty of people:

There was no hope for him this time: it was the third stroke. Night after night I had passed the house (it was vacation time) and studied the lighted square of window: and night after night I had found it lighted in the same way, faintly and evenly. If he was dead, I thought, I would see the reflection of the candles on the darkened blind for I knew that two candles must be set at the head of a corpse (*Dubliners*, 9).

Many of Joyce's Uses of Ideas and Techniques Already Well Explored

On July 25, 1920, James Joyce wrote to his brother Stanislaus, "Odyssey very much in the air here. Anatole France is writing *Le Cyclope*. G. Fauré the musician and opera *Penelope*. Giraudoux has written Elpenor (Paddy Dignam). Guillaume Apollinaire *Les Mamelles de Tirésias.* . . ." (Ellmann, 490).

Interest in the *Odyssey*, however, was not something that had suddenly sprung up. It was evident while Joyce was growing up (he was born in 1882) and when he began to consider using the Ulysses theme—first for a short story and then for a novel—in 1907 (Ellmann, 264, 230). It is clear from Stuart Gilbert's *James Joyce's ULYSSES*, for example, that Joyce had read both Victor Bérard's *Les Phéniciens et l'Odyssée* (1902) and Samuel Butler's *The Authoress of the Odyssey* (1902) (Gilbert, ll, 260 n.; Ellmann, 408). Butler had also translated the *Odyssey* (1900) and the *Iliad* (1898) into colloquial prose, and had written an oratorio entitled *Ulysses* (1904) (Cole, 33, 36).

Much of the interest in Homer was focussed on Ulysses, as Joyce's turned out to be. A study of W. B. Stanford's *The Ulysses Theme* indicates that in the years between 1890 and 1914, over a dozen poems, plays, and novels in which that theme figured importantly were published in England (6), France (2), Italy (4), and Germany (1)—in addition to those listed above. Between 1905 and 1911, three films based on the *Odyssey* and the *Iliad* appeared in Italian: *L'Ile de Calypso*, *La Caduta di Troia*, and *L'Odissea* (Solomon, 66).

Joyce also used other well-explored ideas and techniques. He never would, of course, have called himself a *fumiste*, even if he had heard the term. He saw himself as a genius pioneering new departures in fiction. And, of course, he was. But the shadow plays of Le Chat Noir in the late 1880s and the *Ulysse à Montmartre* of 1910 show clearly that much of Joyce's irreverence toward traditional ideas, attitudes, literary forms and many of the linguistic games he played in *Ulysses* had been well explored over a period of at least twenty years before he began even to make notes for that novel—and certainly before he began to write it. Joyce's genius showed itself in his seeing how what had been explored hit-and-miss in avant-garde literary and intellectual circles could be used in writing a novel —and in his daring to undertake that application.

Thus we have no reports that Joyce subscribed to the battle cry *Épater la bourgeoisie*; but that is exactly what *Ulysses* did. Furthermore, Joyce must have known that it would. If nothing else, his own problems with censorship, which required an eight-year battle for him to publish *Dubliners* (1906-1914), certainly made him aware of how bourgeois tastes controlled publishing. But as Ellmann reports, "Joyce made a point of not understanding the English law, that the printer of objectionable material is as guilty of breaking the law as the publisher, and equally subject to criminal prosecution" (Ellmann, 220). And Joyce underlined that "point" by writing a *Ulysses* in which Leopold Bloom masturbates, Molly describes in graphic detail her romp in the bed with Blazes Boylan, and a very long episode takes place in a bawdy house.

To indicate how much of *Ulysses* might well be characterized as *fumiste*, or, to put it another way, how much of what Joyce "pioneered" in *Ulysses* had already been explored by the avant-garde, we offer the following list of parallels, some major, some trivial, between *Ulysse à Montmartre* and Joyce's *Ulysses*.

Comparison with Joyce's ULYSSES

A reading of the play demonstrates that Joyce and the authors of *Ulysse à Montmartre* shared many attitudes and interests:

1. In both the novel and the play, the contemporary world is juxtaposed—and compared unfavorably—with the ancient Greek world. Just as in *Ulysses*, Mr. Deasy falls considerably short of the Greek Nestor and Molly is no faithful Penelope, so the play points out that the inhabitants of Montmartre do not live up to the standards of such ancients as Plato, Lycurgis, and Praxiteles.

In *The Counterfeiters*, Hugh Kenner argues that such juxtaposition and measurement against classical norms are two of the trends that "finally cauterized" (1910-1930) the effects of the Romantic Interlude. The other two trends were parody and counterfeiting (Kenner, 13-14). Both the French play and Joyce's *Ulysses* parody contemporary norms. Both, finally, are "counterfeits." Of Joyce's first two novels, Kenner says, "Joyce forged an autobiography and then imitated Homer"; and of the second novel he says, "the eighteen sections of *Ulysses* are written in eighteen different styles as though to acknowledge theories of a multiple Homer" (Kenner, 98-99). The French play is also "a counterfeit": it pretends to be a Homeric epic.

2. Neither the novel nor the play makes of Ulysses the hero that Homer does. Although Leopold Bloom stands up to the bullying citizen and befriends hungry gulls, the blind stripling, and an impecunious and defenseless would-be author, he is also in many ways a bumbler. In the French play, a chaste Ulysses in a few seconds first appeals to Minerva to sustain his virtue and then immediately succumbs to the charms of Anthelmys, who needs only her appearance and fewer than sixty words (as summarized by the narrator) to seduce him.

3. Joyce and the play's authors treat respected figures of antiquity with playfulness and even irreverence. Joyce and the play's authors also deliberately treat historical facts carelessly and are sometimes misleadingly—and to the knowledgeable, apparently—imprecise to demonstrate their own cleverness and

to provide enjoyment for the reader/audience. They both, for example, deal with Praxiteles and Zeuxis, icons of art in classical Greece. In *A Portrait*, for example, Stephen argues, "The arts which excite [desire and loathing], pornographic or didactic, are . . . improper arts"; to which Lynch responds, "I told you that one day I wrote my name in pencil on the backside of the Venus of Praxiteles in the Museum. Was that not desire?" (*A Portrait*, 205). Lynch, of course, was being irreverent: to Venus, Praxiteles—and to Stephen. In *Ulysses*, Joyce is playful about Zeuxis. In Hades, Leopold Bloom, looking at a version of the Sacred Heart cut into a tombstone thinks, "Ought to be sideways and red should be painted like a real heart" and then wonders, "Would birds then come and peck like the boy with the basket of fruit but he said no because they ought to have been afraid of the boy. Apollo that was" (*Ulysses*, 6.954-959). Joyce was elaborating a typical Bloomian confusion here. Bloom is apparently mixing Apollo up with the Greek painter Apelles, and is further confusing Apelles with Zeuxis, who, according to Pliny, is supposed to have said, "I have painted the grapes better than the child, and if I had made a success of that as well, the birds would inevitably have been afraid of it" (Thornton, 105).

In the play, the authors use Praxiteles and Zeuxis archly as standards of propriety against whom they measure contemporary artists, who, they say, use pimps and courtesans as models. In the drawing accompanying the stanza, they show three cavorting figures: two well-endowed women with elaborate hairdos, but clad only in black stockings; and a bearded men wearing a flat hat, a garment made of some animal skin, shoes, and leg wrappings suggestive of those worn in classical Greece. The play is disrespectful of Minerva, too (see 4, below). And there are many games played with historical fact. Minerva, for example, takes Anthelmys to Lesbos by train, an amusing anachronism.

4. Like Joyce, the authors of the French "Legende Neo-Grecque" play games with language.

• In *Ulysses*, for example, Joyce uses the Hebrew and Greek alphabets to concoct a telephone number: "Edenville. Aleph, alpha: nought, nought, one" (*Ulysses*, 3.39). In the French play, the authors write of "un grand *beta* qui vend des *Oméga* place du *Delta*" (italics added), where *beta* doubles for the letter in the Greek alphabet and the French word for "blockhead" and Omega is both a Greek letter and trade name of a watch.

• Joyce delights in word echoes and puns: "The Rose Castille. See the wheeze? Rows of cast steel" (*Ulysses*, 7.591); "Pan Poleaxe Paddyrisky (*Ulysses*, 12.565); "See him today at a runefal [funeral] (*Ulysses*, 14.1554); "With all my worldly goods I thee and thou [I thee endow]" (*Ulysses*, 15.375); "We'll manure you, Mr. Flower" (*Ulysses*, 15.32).[5] Similarly, the French authors play on the homophones *salop/salaud* (slut/filthy). They concoct such names as Marquess of Paimboeuf (*pain/boeuf*, bread/meat) and Madame Cent-Kiloi (one hundred kilos, i.e., a fat lady), both a reference to a Marquess Belboeuf. And they play on the word *pallas* (*elle a entendu tout le pallas de Minerve*), using it both as Athena's name and as the French word for "gassy, windy," but also, perhaps, "beautiful" [Marks says "pallas = palas(s)," (Marks, 159)]. At a time when the word games of Marcel Duchamp, Jean-Pierre Brisset, and Raymond Roussel were much admired, such word play is not surprising. We examine many of these word-games in our footnotes to the play.[6]

5. Both the novel and the play make many local references to real contemporary people and to real places. Thus, for example, in the Scylla and Charybdis chapter of *Ulysses*, "the quaker librarian" Thomas William Lyster and the assistant librarian Richard Irvine Best appear (*Ulysses*, 9.1, 15.2244; 9.74), as do Joseph Patrick Nannetti, Dublin printer and Member of Parliament, and the name of the solicitors' firm D. and T.

Fitzgerald (*Ulysses*, 7.121; 7.304), as well as many Dublin streets, pubs, newspapers, etc. In the French play there are direct references to such contemporaries as Paul Escudier, a journalist, and Gustave Binet-Valmer, a novelist and essayist, as well as barely disguised allusions to others like Yon-Lug, one of the singers at Le Chat Noir, and Marquess Belboeuf, the friend of Colette mentioned above—allusions that those who attended the cabaret performances were sure to recognize with chortles.

6. Both the novel and the play also obliterate the boundaries between classical and popular cultures. Readers of *Ulysses* are supposed to keep Telemachus, Ulysses, and Penelope in mind as they read about Stephen, Bloom, and Molly; and in the play, Ulysses lands in a Montmartre which displays many of the characteristics of the Montmartre of 1910. Also, in both the novel and the play, references to classical poets and artists and contemporary references to popular songs, people, and places are inextricably interwoven.

7. Both the novel and the play depend for a good measure of their success, also, on what Kenner calls "connoisseurship":

Antiques were once sought out because they embodied a timeless authority of design supposed to be no longer attainable (Chippendale, Sheraton; and compare the finality of Egyptian sculpture). They are now prized just when no such claims are to be plausibly made for them; only that in some former pocket of time they were purposeful (stained glass lampshades, French telephones; and compare the rectitude of the Cigar Store Indian). This phenomenon is less obscure than its analysts, who circulate the impenetrable term "camp." The artifacts are stylistic quotations; the environment they create is a cultural echo-chamber, reverberant with amusing scraps of dead languages. Things are utterances (Kenner, xii).

Much of the enjoyment in both the novel and the play derives from the classical and contemporary references and from familiarity with the slang of the particular subcultures. Many a resident of early twentieth-century Dublin would have understood *Ulysses* in a way that a twenty-first-century American cannot without such aids as Weldon Thornton's *Allusions in ULYSSES* and Gifford and Seidman's *ULYSSES Annotated*. Similarly, many residents of early twentieth-century Paris would have gone to La Lune Rousse equipped with the knowledge which would have allowed them to chortle over the classical and contemporary allusions in *Ulysse à Montmartre*. We hope that our analysis here and our footnotes to the play will enable contemporary Americans to respond to that French play in the same way—as connoisseurs.

In both the novel and the play, therefore, myth, history, and contemporary fact are threads woven into the fabric of a new work of literature to produce new figures on a new ground: new perspectives and new juxtapositions to make new comments on the classical and contemporary worlds. Language is similarly rethought, reconfigured, played with to construct that text. The knowledgeable audience of the resultant texts extract from those texts comments on both the classical world and on the version of the contemporary world that the author is building for them: for the novel, turn-of-the-century Dublin in all its variety;[7] for the play, a shorter text and thus, appropriately, a smaller geographic area and subculture, turn-of-the-century Montmartre.

8. In both the novel and the play, the authors avoid explicit judgments on important social matters. In *Ulysses*, for example, while readers prefer Leopold Bloom to the citizen, their evaluations of Stephen, Bloom, and Molly vary widely—even wildly. That is only possible because Joyce's judgments about them are not evident in the text—even though he made explicit statements about those in conversations with his friends.[8] In the play, similarly, while the authors make fun of the writers and artists with whom they are associated, they do not pass explicit judgment about the life of the Montmartrian subculture. Nor do they indicate any preference between the

proposed lesbianism of Anthelmys, who is taken (by train!) to Lesbos and the heterosexuality of the other women of Montmartre, who are left with rounded bellies as "souvenirs" of the stay of Ulysses' companions. There is little didacticism in either work.

9. In both the play and the novel, women comment on the male brutality and selfishness in lovemaking. In the play, Minerva warns Anthelmys graphically against the violence of Ulysses' lust, concluding with statement, "You see! It is like this for a man: / For him the woman is always / Nothing but an animal to sleep with." In *Ulysses*, Molly comments on Boylan's "tremendous red brute of a thing": "like a Stallion driving it up into you because that's all they want out of you with that determined vicious look in his eyes" (*Ulysses*, 18.144, 152).

10. Both works suggest lesbianism. In the play Minerva takes Anthelmys away "to catch the train to Lesbos . . . an island of divine happiness where a kiss lingers and a caress has no end." In the novel, Molly remembers Hester Stanhope amorously— "the night of the storm I slept in her bed she had her arms around me then we were fighting in the morning with the pillow what fun" (*Ulysses* 18.612-624, 638-643).

11. Both also have scatalogical references. In the play the ambiguous statement "As they say in the synagogue . . . Cahen-caha" suggests *caca*, the term French children use for excrement, to which Parisiens would be attuned at the height of the anti-semitism due to the Dreyfus affair (Cate, 55). In the novel, Bloom sits down in the outhouse, defecates, and wipes himself with a page from *Titbits* (*Ulysses*, 4.460, 500-540).

12. The play takes place primarily in the red-light district. In the novel, the longest—and perhaps the most revealing— chapter, Circe, takes place in Dublin's red-light district.

There are other parallels of less importance, some to be expected because of the Greek origin of the Ulysses theme, and some not.

• Joyce makes important use of the Daedalus/Icarus story, both in *A Portrait of the Artist as a Young Man* and in *Ulysses* (*Ulysses*, 9.953). In the French play, Ulysses and his men arrive in Montmartre on a holiday dedicated to Icarus and his Daedalian machine, perhaps, as we explain in a footnote to the play, because aviation and two aviators in particular were very much in the news when the play was put on in Paris (September, 1910).

• Ulysses refers to many of the places and characters in Greek myth that the French play does: nymphs (*Ulysses*, 4.369), Achilles (*Ulysses*, 9.350, etc.), Ajax (*Ulysses*, 15.709), Attica (*Ulysses*, 10.1073), Circe (*Ulysses*, 15.2091), Croesus (*Ulysses*, 15.3004), Éphebe (*Ulysses*, 9.531), Glycere (*Ulysses*, 14.1156), Ithaca (*Ulysses*, 7.1034), Mercury (*Ulysses*, 1.601), Neptune (*Ulysses*, 7.245), Pallas Anthena (*Ulysses*, 9.876), Penelope (*Ulysses*, 7.1039), Pygmalion (*Ulysses*, 8.924), Sirens (*Ulysses*, 16.1813, etc.), Troy (*Ulysses*, 8.392, etc.), Venus (*Ulysses*, 9.249, etc.).[9] Both use the word umbrella in a context suggesting contraceptives (*Ulysses*, 14.785); the play: *s'il veut transformer en pluie d'or, elle promet de ne pas prendre de parapluie* (if he will transform himself into golden rain, she will promise to take out an umbrella).

• Both works make reference to the worldly appetites of Jupiter. In the play Anthelmys reminds Ulysses "that Ulysses was above all a god who in order to satisfy women would turn himself into a swan or a bull." In *Ulysses* Joyce makes only passing reference to the story of Leda and the Swan (*Ulysses*, 12.283); in Scylla and Carybdis, Stephen invokes Jove's interest in sexual activities ("Jove, a cool ruttime send them") (*Ulysses*, 9.539);

and in Oxen of the Son, there is a talk of a gelded bull much admired by Irish women that may carry ironic overtones of the stories of Jupiter assuming animal shapes to copulate with women (*Ulysses*, 14.575-646). In his notesheets for *Ulysses*, however, Joyce showed greater interest in Jupiter's sexual appetites. On the sheet that Herring characterizes as Circe 1, Joyce wrote "Jupiter is an animal" and on Circe 3, "Golden rain: Jove fucked Alcmene as Amphytrion for 3 long days when he came she knew. Tiresias revealed last mortal fucked by Jove" (Herring, 268.97, 282.125).

• In both the novel and the play, a whore attempts to seduce Ulysses and fails. In *Ulysses* Zoe tries to attract Bloom (*Ulysses*, 15.1279-1344), but he does not succumb. In the play Ulysses succumbs, but Minerva intervenes by whisking Anthelmys off to Lesbos.

There are other even more incidental parallels:

• Both the novel and the play have boys from high school appearing in nighttown (*Ulysses*, 15.1404).

• Both madams are large women (*Ulysses*, 15.2742, 2753).

• Both the novel and the play refer to Mountjoy (*Ulysses*, 10.12, 41, 54, etc.).

• Both the novel and the play mention aphrodisiacs (*Ulysses*, 15.2736).

Readers of the play, our translation of which follows this discussion, will undoubtedly find other parallels between *Ulysses* and *Ulysse à Montmartre*. We wish them success.

Readers will also find many differences between *Ulysses* and the French play. The play is slight—an entertainment, unlike the novel, which is considered one of the major achievements of the twentieth century. Telemachus and Penelope do not appear in the play in any guise. The novel and the play also present an entirely different Ulysses. The Ulysses in the play is easily manipulated by the madame of the brothel, for example. That is true for a while of Bloom in "Circe," but ultimately he extricates himself and Stephen firmly and puts the madame in her place. The play shows a mythical hero as an incompetent. The novel shows an ordinary man survive by sincerity, cunning, and perseverance—some of the important characteristics of Homer's Ulysses. Indeed, some critics have argued that Bloom achieves a mythical status in today's world, that he is both a contemporary Everyman and a contemporary Ulysses. There are, of course, many other important differences—too many to even list.

Conclusion

In our comparison of the novel and the play, we do not intend to equate them—either to denigrate the novel by making the play more important than it is or to elevate the play by associating it with the novel. The record shows that Joyce took years to write the novel: he jotted down voluminous notes, wrote and rewrote in longhand, added to the typescript, and scrawled long additions in the margins of the galleys. We suspect that the writing of the play was akin to the writing of a television script by three gag writers or to a session of a jazz trio, in which each player picks up a theme begun by one of the group and embellishes it or tries new variations on it, to the amusement and encouragement of the others.

The play is interesting in itself because it brings back however briefly turn-of-the-century Montmartre. But it caught our attention and invited our energies largely because it shows that much of what appears in *Ulysses* was "in the air" at the time. What Joyce did with those interests shows his artistry. *Ulysse à*

Montmartre is a skit, intended to draw quick laughs from a knowing audience, to amuse for an evening. It is not mentioned in any of the books we have read about La Belle Époque. Although it was published by the press established to advertise the cabaret La Lune Rousse, its first performance may well have been its last. *Ulysses*, however, is a work of literature rich enough to have invited continued and growing attention.

Notes to the Essay

1. We assume that the play was published at the time the play was put on or soon thereafter. Since we translated this play for purposes of scholarship rather than performance, our translation is rather literal. It may as a result seem wooden; but we wanted our English text to differ as little as possible from the French. Some sentences are awkward, for example, because we maintained the number of lines in each stanza of the original and translated line for line rather than rearranging for smoother reading. Similarly, our punctuation follows the original, which is sometimes erratic.

2. The original says, *Montmartre fut découvert par les Grecs voici bientot trois mille ans*—"Montmartre was discovered by the Greeks over three thousand years ago." Since the French *découvert* means both "uncovered" and "discovered," the original carries a suggestion that the English translation does not: the Greeks picked up a rock and underneath they found. . . " The sentence is a further wry comment by the authors on not only Montmartre but all of France, since the Montmartre that Ulysses and his men uncovered/discovered, was, according to the play, not a barren area, but rather well populated by French residents of the time. The word play is typical of much of the play.

3. See also Huizinga's discussion of the relationship between poetry and playfulness and poetry and the riddle (134-135), which is relevant to the use of language in both the play and the novel. The emphasis of contemporary students of Greek myth on its fluidity and improvisatory character is also relevant to the way modern authors treat such myths, as they make them serve their own—modern—purposes: "Mythology, then, was an open-ended system. As has been pointed out recently, it is precisely this improvisatory character of myth that guarantees its centrality in Greek religion. "It is not bound to forms hardened and stiffened by canonical authority, but mobile, fluent and free to respond to a changing experience of the world" (Bremmer, "What is Greek Myth?", *Interpretations of Greek Mythology*, ed. 3-4). Bremmer is quoting J. Gould, "On Making Sense of Greek Religion," in *Greek Religion and Society*, ed. P. Easterling and J.V. Muir, 8.

4. Stanislaus says, "while we were living at Windsor Terrace" (Stanislaus Joyce, 90).

5. *Finnegans Wake*, of course, carries this interest even further. For Joyce's use of multilingual puns, for example, see Ellmann, 546.

6. Some of the puns we explore in our footnotes to our translation may seem extravagant fictions of our imagination. But French writers of the time were playing such games with language. For example, in 1890 Jean-Pierre Brisset published *La Science de Dieu*, in which he played with a group of phrases which sounded very much alike: *l'eau j'ai, l'haut j'ai, l'os jai, le au jet, l'eau jet, loge ai, lot j'ai, lauge ai*. The book was reprinted in 1900 and reappeared in 1913 under the title *Les Origines Humaines* (Brisset, 10). Raymond Roussel wrote poems and fiction in which he played with language in similar ways. He explained his "metagrams" this way: "I chose two words almost alike. . . . For example, "billard" and "pillard." Then I added to each of them similar words but in two different senses, and I thus obtained almost identical phrases" (Roussel, 11-12). Similarly, in one of his poems appears the following pair of lines:

Avec un parti pri de rudesse ses gens . . . .
Ave coté part type rit des rues d'essai suage. En
(type des rues ri d'essai suage) (Roussel, 24).

Marcel Duchamp, who some years later published columns of puns under the pseudonym Rose Selavy, (*Érôs c'est la vie*) said that "Brisset and Roussel were the two men in those years whom I most admired for their delerium of imagination" (Sweeney, 19-20; reprinted in Chipp, 394-395). These experiments led to the even more extravagant word games played by the Dadaists who gathered at the Cabaret Voltaire in Zurich in the spring of

1916. In trying to understand the play, we tried to read references and phrases with "imagination"—we hope, however, not to delerium. For a discussion of these phenomena and their relationship to Joyce, see Steinberg, 277-298.

7. Joyce told Frank Budgen, "I want to give a picture of Dublin so complete that if the city one day suddenly disappeared from the earth it could be reconstructed out of my book" (Budgen, 67-68; see also Ellmann, 363-369).

8. See, for example, Joyce's comments to Budgen on Leopold Bloom (Budgen, 115-116).

9. Here and below we give only the *Ulysses* references since the occurrences in *Ulysse à Montmartre* are readily apparent on the first reading.

Bibliography

Appignanesi, Lisa. *The Cabaret*. New York: University Books, 1976.

Avery, Catherine, ed. *The New Century Classical Handbook*. New York: Appleton CenturyCrofts, 1962.

Bairati, Eleonora, et al., *La Belle Époque*. New York: William Morrow, 1962.

Bayard, Jean-Émile. *Montmarte Past and Present*. New York: Brentano's, 1925.

Bonnaud, Dominique, Lucien Boyer, and Numa Blès. *Ulysse à Montmarte*. Paris: Logiz de la Lune Rousse, 1910.

Bremmer, Jan. "What is Greek Myth." In *Interpretations of Greek Mythology*, Ed. Jan Bremmer. London: Groom Helm, 1987.

Brisset, Jean-Pierre. *La Science de Dieu*. Paris: Chamuel, 1900.

Budgen, Frank. *James Joyce and the Making of Ulysses*. New York: Harrison Smith and Robert Hass, 1935.

Carco, Francis. *The Last Bohemia: From Montmartre to the Quartier Latin*. Trans. Madeleine Boyd. New York: Henry Holt & Co., 1928.

Cate, Phillip Dennis and Mary Shaw, eds. *The Spirit of Montmartre: Cabarets, Humor, and the Avant-Garde, 1875-1905*. New Brunswick, Jane Voorhees Zimmerli Art Museum, 1996.

Chipp, Herschel. *Theories of Modern Art*. Berkeley: University of California Press, 1968.

Cole, G. D. H. *Samuel Butler*. London: Longmans, Green, & Co., 1961.

Courthion, Pierre. *Montmartre*. Geneva: Skira, 1956.

Dussane, Béatrix. *Dieux des Planches*. Paris: Flammarion, 1964.

Ellmann, Richard. *James Joyce*. New York: Oxford University Press, 1982.

Garner, Philippe, ed. *The Encyclopedia of Decorative Arts 1890-1940*. New York: Galahad Books, 1982.

Gifford, Don, Robert J. Seidman. *Ulysses Annotated: Notes for Joyce's "Ulysses."* Berkeley: University of California Press, 1988.

Gilbert, Stuart. *James Joyce's "Ulysses."* New York: Alfred A. Knopf, 1952.

Greenwald, Harold. *The Prostitute in Literature*. Ed. Aron Krich. New York: Ballantine Books, 1960.

Hartnoll, Phyllis, ed. *The Oxford Companion to the Theatre*, 4th ed. London: Oxford University Press, 1983.

Herbert, Michel. *La Chanson à Montmartre*. Paris: La Table Ronde, 1967.

Herring, Philip. *Joyce's "Ulysses" Notesheets in the British Museum*. Charlottesville: University of Virginia Press, 1972.

Honour, Hugh. *The Image of the Black in Western Art*. Volume One. Cambridge: Harvard University Press, 1989.

Huizinga, Johan. *Homo Ludens*. Boston: Beacon Press, 1950.

Jeanne, Paul. *Les Théâtres d'Ombres à Montmartre de 1887 à 1923*. Paris: Les Éditions des Presses Modernes au Palais-Royal, 1937.

Joyce, James. *Dubliners*. New York: Viking, 1969.

Joyce, James. *A Portrait of the Artist as a Young Man*. Ed. Chester G. Anderson. New York: Viking, 1969.

Joyce, James. *Ulysses*. Ed. Hans Walter Gabler. New York: Random House, 1986.

Joyce, Stanislaus. *My Brother's Keeper*. New York: Viking, 1958.

Jullian, Philippe. *Montmartre*. Trans. Anne Carter. Oxford: Phaidon; New York: E. P. Dutton, 1977.

Kenner, Hugh. *The Counterfeiters: An Historical Comedy*. Baltimore: Johns Hopkins University Press, 1985.

La Grande Encyclopédie. Paris: Librairie Larousse, 1973.

Larousse du XXe Siècle. Paris: Librairie Larousse, 1928.

Lemaître, Jules. *Theatrical Impressions*. Trans. Frederic Whyte. Port Washington: Kennikat Press, 1970.

Littlewood, Ian. *Paris: A Literary Companion*. London: John Murray, 1987.

Marks, Joseph. *The New French-English Dictionary of Slang and Colloquialisms*. Rev. Georgette A. Marks and Albert J. Farmer. New York: E. P. Dutton, 1971.

Oreglia, Giacomo. *The Commedia dell'Arte*. Trans. Lovett F. Edwards. New York: Hill & Wang, 1968.

Rearick, Charles. *Pleasures of the Belle Époque: Entertainment & Festivity in the Turn-of-the-Century France.* New Haven: Yale University Press, 1985.

Roussel, Raymond. *Comment j'al écrit certain de mes livres.* Paris: Pauvert, 1963.

Rudorff, Raymond. *Belle Époque – Paris in the Nineties.* London: Hamish Hamilton, 1972.

Segel, Harold B. *Turn-of-the-Century Cabaret.* New York: University of Columbia Press, 1987.

Siegel, Jerrold E. *Bohemian Paris.* New York: Viking, 1986.

Solomon, Jon. *The Ancient World of the Cinema.* New York: A. S. Barnes, 1978.

Stanford, W. B. *The Ulysses Theme.* Oxford: Basil Blackwell, 1963.

Steinberg, Erwin R. *The Stream of Consciousness and Beyond in "Ulysses."* Pittsburgh: University of Pittsburgh Press, 1973.

Sweeney, James Johnson. *Eleven Europeans in America.* Bulletin of the Museum of Modern Art 13, nos. 4-5. Reprinted from Chipp. See entry.

Weldon, Thornton. *Allusions in "Ulysses": An Annotated List.* Chapel Hill: University of North Carolina Press, 1968.

Wachsmann, Klaus. *Cabaret* in *Grove Dictionary of Music and Musicians.* New York: Macmillan, 1985.

Ulysse à Montmartre
D. Bonnaud
Numa Blès
L. Boyer

D. Bonnaud, Numa Blès & L. Boyer

❖ ❖ ❖

Ulysse à Montmartre

LÉGENDE NÉO-GRECQUE
EN UN PROLOGUE & TROIS TABLEAUX

Dessins de GIFFEY ❖ *Décors de GYANINY*

Présentée pour la première fois au Théâtre d'Ombres
du " Logiz de la Lune Rousse "
le 9 Septembre 1910

Société d'Éditions de "LA LUNE ROUSSE"
34 & 36, BOULEVARD DE CLICHY
PARIS

D. Bonnaud, Numa Blès & L. Boyer

❧ ❧ ❧

Ulysses in Montmartre

A NEO-GREEK LEGEND
IN A PROLOGUE & THREE TABLEAUS

Drawings by GIFFEY   ❧   *Sets by GYANINY*

Presented for the first time at the Théâtre d'Ombres
of "Logiz de la Lune Rousse"
on September 9, 1910

Originally Published by

Société d'Éditions de "LA LUNE ROUSSE"
34 & 36, BOULEVARD DE CLICHY
PARIS

Ulysse à Montmartre

LÉGENDE NÉO-GRECQUE
EN UN PROLOGUE ET TROIS TABLEAUX

*présentée pour la première fois au Théâtre d'Ombres
de "LA LUNE ROUSSE" le 9 Septembre 1910*

❊ ❊ ❊

Le récitant :   Numa Blès

Soli et chœurs par :   D. Bonnaud, Lucien Boyer,
                                              P. Weil, G. Baltha,
                                                      V. Tourtal
                                         et Mⁱⁱᵉ Lucy Pezet

L'ingénieur-machiniste :   J. Bondenat

Au piano :   le compositeur Adolf Stanislas

❊ ❊ ❊

REPRODUCTIONS PHOTOGRAPHIQUES DE M. CH. MARTIN
179 bis, avenue de Versailles

Ulysses in Montmartre

A NEO-GREEK LEGEND
IN A PROLOGUE AND THREE TABLEAUS

*Presented for the first time at the Shadow Theatre
of La Lune Rousse on September 9, 1910*

❖ ❖ ❖

The Narrator:	Numa Blès
Solo Singers and Choir:	D. Bonnaud, Lucien Boyer, P. Weil, G. Baltha, V. Tourtal and Miss Lucy Pezet
Technical Director:	J. Bondenat
At the Piano:	the Composer Adolf Stanislas

❖ ❖ ❖

PHOTOGRAPHIC REPRODUCTIONS BY MR. CH. MARTIN
179 Avenue de Versailles

Ulysse à Montmartre

PROLOGUE

LE RÉCITANT

Mesdames, Mes Gentilshommes,

Montmartre n'a pas été découvert, comme on le croit communément, par M. Paul Escudier. Montmartre fut découvert par les Grecs voici bientôt trois mille ans, et cela ne nous rajeunit pas. Il était réservé au plus avisé des héros d'Homère, au subtil Ulysse, de découvrir cette Butte fameuse où sa vertu devait, — comme vous allez le voir par la suite, — trébucher pour la première fois.

En ce temps-là le sage Ulysse,
Tenté par les dieux ennemis,
N'admettait en fait de délice
Que celui par l'hymen permis.

C'est en vain que des nymphes roses,
Des naïades aux frais appas
Lui montraient des choses, des choses....
Notre Ulysse ne marchait pas !

Ulysses in Montmartre

PROLOGUE

THE NARRATOR

Ladies and Gentlemen,

Montmartre was not discovered as it is commonly believed by Mr. Paul Escudier.[1] Montmartre was discovered by the Greeks over three thousand years ago, and we haven't rediscovered that. Such credit must go to the shrewdest of Homer's heroes, to the subtle Ulysses,[2] for discovering this famous hill where his virtue, as you will see later, was to be tested for the first time.

At that time the wise Ulysses,
Tempted by warring gods,
Was not permitted the joy of happiness
Which matrimony provided.

It was in vain that the rosy nymphs,
The Naiades with their sweet charms[3]
Showed him things, things. . . .
Our Ulysses couldn't take part!

C'est en vain qu'au bord des Cyclades
Les Sirènes tendaient leurs bras
Vers Ulysse et ses camarades :
Eux marchaient; lui ne marchait pas !

Même il coupa court à l'églogue
De la tendre Nausicaa
— Comme on dit à la synagogue —
En s'en allant Cahen-caha ;

Circé qui faisait du plus sage
Un petit goret folichon,
Malgré tout son cœur à l'ouvrage,
Ne fit pas d'Ulysse un cochon ;

Parfois la femme de son hôte
— L'usage a d'ailleurs survécu —
L'incitait à la douce faute
De faire son mari cocu,

Mais si d'un geste trop extrême
La dame corsait l'entretien,
Ulysse rentrait en lui-même :
Il ne répondait rien, rien, rien ;

Si la dame insistait, folâtre,
Il lui servait alors, tout frais,
Le cliché banal du théâtre :
« Impossible ! Mille regrets !

Aimer quelque nymphe interlope
Serait un coup des plus vilains
Cependant que ma Pénélope
Travaille pour les Gobelins. »

De cette chasteté bizarre
Chacun s'étonnait à l'envi :
Ne lisait-il que du Pindare
Edité par Calmann-Lévy ?

In vain on the banks of the Cyclades[4]
The Sirens extended their arms[5]
Toward Ulysses and his companions:
They accepted; but not he!

He even cut short the eclogue
Of sweet Nausicaa[6]
—As they say in the synagogue—[7]
Vanishing Cahen-caha;

Circé more wisely[8]
Offered him a frolicsome piglet,
Yet in spite of his desire for it,
It was not fitting for Ulysses to have a pig;

Often the wife of his host
—Using the term rather loosely—
Would offer her favors
To cuckold her husband,

But if with behaviour too extreme
The lady ardently tempted him,
Ulysses withdrew to himself:
He responded not at all, not at all;

If the lady insisted, playfully
He would then return, quite readily,
To the banal cliché of the theatre:
"Impossible! A thousand regrets!

To love some intruding nymph
Would be too villainous an act
While my Pénélope[9]
Is busy with her tapestry."

For such a peculiar chastity
Everyone is envious and amazed:
Couldn't such a thing be read only in Pindar[10]
As published by Calmann-Lévy?[11]

Pour narguer chaque courtisane
Malgré ses parfums et son fard
Usait-il de quelque tisane
Half and half camphre et nénuphar ?

Pour dompter ainsi la nature
Quel pouvait être son moyen ?
Portait-il sur lui la ceinture
Du pharmacope Gallien ?

Prenait-il quelque panacée
Quand par hasard il se sentait ?...
Cela n'est pas dans l'*Odyssée*,
Homère là-dessus se tait.

❊ ❊ ❊

Si, rebelle à tous les dictames,
Le sage Ulysse restait coi,
La raison en est que ces dames
N'avaient pas le « je ne sais quoi »,

Le chic, le « chien », le savoir-faire,
Qu'on trouve au pays Montmartrois
Où la plus modeste bergère
Est un morceau digne des rois.

C'est pourquoi Vénus, mécontente,
Dit un jour à ce vieux Jupin :
« Toutes les fois que je le tente
Ulysse me pose un lapin !

Cet homme a des ruses de martre
Pour se soustraire à mon pouvoir....
Allons, faites donner Montmartre !
Nous allons voir ! Nous allons voir !...»

To fend off every courtesan
In spite of her perfumes and make-up
Applied with some herbs
Half and half camphor and waterlily?

To subdue thus the urges of nature
What could be his method?
Could he wear a chastity belt
As prescribed by the great doctor Galen?[12]

Would he take it as a relief
When by accident he would feel the urge? . . .
That is not in the *Odyssey*,
Homer held it back.

❊ ❊ ❊

Yes, rebel against all solutions,
The wise Ulysses stayed calm,
The reason is that all these ladies
Don't have "what it takes."

The slick, the "bitch," and the trick,
That one finds in Montmartre land
Where the most modest shepherd
Is worthy to be a king.

This is why Venus, unhappy,[13]
Said one day to old Man Jupe:[14]
"Every time I try to seduce him
This Ulysses is elusive as a rabbit!

This man has the cunning of a fox
So to strengthen my power over him. . . .
Let's get him to Montmartre!
And let's see! Let's see! . . . "

PREMIER TABLEAU

L'arrivée d' Ulysse

———

LE RÉCITANT

Et c'est ainsi que vers l'an 1000 avant Jésus-Christ les guetteurs aux yeux d'argus qui surveillaient les rives séquanaises virent arriver des trirèmes d'un modèle encore inconnu.

Ces trirèmes abordèrent au pied de la Butte Sacrée, car cette année-là la Seine avait débordé, inondant la moitié de la ville et noyant l'autre moitié, ce qui fait qu'à la fin du compte tout le monde était... submergé.

FIRST TABLEAU

The Arrival of Ulysses

THE NARRATOR

Thus it happened that around the year 1000 before Jesus Christ the lookout men with their sharp eyes who watch the banks of the Seine saw the arrival of a model of the triremes not known before.

These triremes landed at the foot of the sacred hill, for that year the Seine had flooded, inundating half of the city and drowning the other half, so that when the final count was taken everyone was . . . submerged.

49

Une Commission avait été nommée pour empêcher le retour d'un pareil désastre, et nous savons qu'elle fonctionne encore.

Au loin, des chants s'élèvent des trirèmes :

LE CHŒUR

Air: *La Mer*, d'Adolf Stanislas.

Yo ! yo ! yo !
Salut, rive nouvelle
Où Pallas immortelle
A conduit nos vaisseaux !
Vers la rive propice
Que ta trirème glisse !..
Puisses-tu, sage Ulysse,
Voir la fin de tes maux !

LE RÉCITANT

Les trirèmes d'Ulysse ont ,abordé, et les naturels de Paris regardent avec curiosité ces navires qui viennent d'Ilion par la mer Méditerranée — Paris-Ilion-Méditerranée !..

Ulysse aborde à Montmartre un jour de féte où Icare, l'aviateur fameux, doit essayer son moteur Dédale, d'un cheval-icare, et tenter de boucler le Circuit de la Gaule, — épreuve jusque-là réservée aux dames.

Le populaire afflue.

A committee was formed to prevent the return of a similar disaster, and we know that this committee continues to work at it.

From faraway rose songs from the triremes:

THE CHORUS

After the tune of *La Mer*, by Adolf Stanislas.

Yo! yo! yo!
Hail, new bank
Where the immortal Pallas
Has guided our vessels!
Toward the propitious bank
That the trireme glides! . . .
You can, cunning Ulysses,
See the end of all your troubles!

THE NARRATOR

The triremes of Ulysses landed and the inhabitants of Paris watched with curiosity these ships which come from Ilion by way of the Mediterranean—Paris—Ilion—Mediterranean!. .[15]

Ulysses lands in Montmartre on a festive day when Icarus,[16] the famous aviator, has to try his Daedalin machine, a winged-horse,[17] in an attempt to cover the Circuit de la Gaule, —a custom reserved until then for women.

People arrive in droves.

C'est d'abord la famille du brave horloger Eukrêtinos, un grand bêta qui vend des Oméga place du Delta, assis sur un tapis d'alpha. Il est dans tous ses êta !..

Une jeune apprentie, arpettaz, de la maison Crouzeix, Reboux ou Viros. Elle court chez le pâtissier voisin, Bilitis, dont elle apprécie les célèbres chaussons aux pommes : les chaussons de Bilitis.

Quelques gosses, loupioï, qu'on croirait dessinés par Poulboss, et qui manifestent leur contentement en brandissant des lanternes corinthiennes.

Un vendeur d'éphéméris passe en criant des titres sensationnels:

(Dans le théâtre) : Demandez !.. Dernières nouvelles... La prise de Troie... L'arrestalion de Priam... Le satyre de l'Acropole !.. Horribles détails !

Calicos, chef du rayon des clamydes à Pygmalion, le grand magasin qui vient encore de s'agrandir pour faire concurrence aux Galeries Thucydide.

Madame Cent-Kiloï, qui joue les Diane d'Ephèse à Bobinos. Elle semble sculptée par quelque coroplaste d'Egine ou de Tanagra :

Egine par devant, Tanagra par derrière. Ses charmes abondants séduisent Calicos qui em-boîte le pas à cette callypige, mais avec appréhension, car il a peur callypige son portemonnaie, — to pognon.

First it is the family of the courageous watchmaker Eukrêtinos,[18] a great Beta[19] who sells Omega at Delta Square, sitting on an Alpha carpet. He is spread out everywhere! . . .

Then comes a young milliner's apprentice of the House of Crouzeix,[20] Reboux[21] or Viros.[22] She runs toward Bilitis, the neighboring pastry shop, where she always enjoys the famous apple turnovers: the turnovers of Bilitis.[23]

Some bratty girls come in, as if in a drawing by Poulboss,[24] who show their satisfaction by brandishing Corinthian lamps.[25]

A peddler of ephemera passes calling out sensational titles:

(In the theatre): Buy! . . . The latest news . . . . The capture of Troy . . . . The arrest of Priam . . . .[26] The satyr of the Acropolis! . . . Horrible details!

Calicos[27] [appears], the head of the capes department at Pygmalion,[28] the great store which just got larger by a merger with the Galleries of Thucydides.[29]

[And then there is] Madame Hundred Kilos,[30] who plays the character of Diana[31] of Ephesus at the Bobinos.[32] She looks as if she was sculpted in a relief by Egine[33] or Tanagra:[34]

Egine for the front, Tanagra for the back. Her abundant charms seduce Calicos, who falls in step with these well-shaped asses, yet with apprehension, for he is afraid to draw attention to his derriere in case his pocket will be picked and he will lose his dough.

Une petite bonne et son hoplite :

L'hoplite Agathos, bon, brave à la guerre ; et la bonne Agathé, brave, bonne à tout faire.

Un hippo taxi, — de hippo : voiture, et taxi : cheval, — conduit par le cocher Automédon qui connut des jours plus glorieux et conduisit jadis le fameux quadrige du Moulin-Rouge.

Eyrénès Fulakoï, que les Athéniens appelaient irrévérencieusement Sergoï, et qui précèdent la Philarmonia du XVIIIe arrondissement, —laquelle joue ses airs les plus populaires : « *Mikra Britanna* » (la petite Bretonne) ; « *Ouk ekeï riflardon* » (Il n'a pas de parapluie) ; « *Eké, Poupoulous !* » (Viens, Poupoule !) et autres hymnes nationaux, œuvres du poète Tyrtée.

✻ ✻ ✻

Mais Ulysse est descendu à terre avec ses compagnons et son porte-bagages. Il cherche un guide qui lui révèle les beautés de ce pays inconnu, et le hasard amène sur ses pas le chansonnier Yon-Lugas... A sa coupe de cheveux plutôt négligée, Ulysse a reconnu un poète.

[Then comes] a little maid with her bodyguard:

The bodyguard [was] a soldier named Agathos, good, courageous at war; and the maid, whose name was Agatha, was also courageous and good at everything.[35]

A little horse-drawn cab,[36]—carriage and taxi: horse—driven by a coachman named Automédon who lived through glorious days and was in charge of driving the famous chariot of the Moulin Rouge.

[Here is] Eyrénès Fulakoï,[37] whom the Athenians call irreverently Sergoï[38] and who marches in front of the Philharmonic band of the 18th district,—which plays the most popular tunes such as: "*Mikra Britanna*" (The little girl from Bretany); "*Ouk ekeï riflardon*" (He has no umbrella); "*Eké, Poupoulous!*" (Come on, Poupoule!)[39] and other national hymns, works of the poet Tyrtée.[40]

* * *

However, Ulysses has landed with his companions and his suitcases. He looks for a guide who will show him the beauty of this unknown country, and chance leads him to Yon-Lugas, the singer . . . [41] By his unkempt hair, Ulysses recognized a poet.

Il congédie ses compagnons, renvoie son porte-bagages à *l'hôtel du Péloponèse et des Voyageurs réunis*, et s'adressant à Yon-Lugas :

— « O poète à la barbe inculte, dit-il, apprends-moi quelle est cette contrée, quels en sont les dieux, les mœurs et les principaux habitants ! »

Et le poète, ayant accordé sa lyre et bu préalablement quelques amer-kurakoï, s'exprime en ces termes dans son idiome natal :

O guerrier qui nous viens d'Ithaque,
Ayant subi la rude attaque
Des vents et des flots en courroux,
Ah ! rends grâces à la fortune
Qui t'a conduit malgré Neptune
Vers ces bords accueillants et doux :

Ici, sache-le, c'est Montmartre
Où jamais l'ennui, cette dartre,
Ne marqua les fronts d'un pli lourd ;
Ici, c'est Montmartre-Montjoie,
C'est la colline de la joie,
C'est la colline de l'amour !

He dismisses his companions, and sends his suitcases to *The Hotel of the Peloponeses and the Reunited Voyagers*,[42] and he addresses Yon-Lugas:

—"O poet with the wild beard," says he, "tell me what is this country, what are its gods, its customs, and its principal inhabitants!"

So the poet, holding up his lyre and drinking beforehand a bitter drink, expounds himself in his native idiom:

O warrior who comes to us from Ithaca,
Having sustained the violent attacks
Of winds, tides of wrath,
Ah! blessed be the fortune
Which guided you despite Neptune[43]
Toward these quiet and sweet shores:

Here, such a place, is Montmartre[44]
Where never is boredom, such eruption,
Doesn't show on worried foreheads;
Here is Montmartre-Mountjoy,[45]
This is the hill of pleasure,
This is the hill of love![46]

Je te sais de vertu rigide,
Mais, puisque tu m'as pris pour guide,
Ulysse, tu m'écouteras ;
Sans rien craindre, regarde, observe !
D'ailleurs, protégé par Minerve,
Je sais que tu résisteras.

Tu peux constater que la mode
Des femmes n'est point incommode,
Que leur corps n'est pas ligoté :
Leurs seins ignorent le corsage
Et, tels des chevaux de dressage,
Se présentent en liberté.

Je vois que ta pudeur s'indigne :
Ça manque de feuilles de vigne ?
Mais qu'est-ce que tu veux, mon cher !
C'est en vain que tu te révoltes :
La pluie a gâté nos récoltes,
La feuille de vigne est très cher.

Voici venir un exemplaire
De cette espèce séculaire
Que l'on nomme d'un nom flatteur,
Car toujours les femmes qu'ils suivent,
Ainsi que les locomotives,
Ont derrière elles leur... tender.

I know of your rigid virtue,
But, since you have taken me as a guide,
Ulysses, listen to me;
Without fear, look, observe!
Otherwise, protégé of Minerva,[47]
I know that you will resist.

You can see that women's fashion
Is not in the least uncomfortable,
That their bodies are not firmly bound:
And their breasts overflow the bodice
And, like horses in training,
Show off without inhibition.

I see that your sense of decency is shocked:
You miss the fig leaves?
But what do you want, my friend!
You resist in vain:
For the rain has damaged our harvest,
Fig leaves are truly very scarce.

Here comes a specimen
Of the time-honored kind
Whom one calls flatterer,
For always women follow them,
Like locomotives,
Are followed by their . . . tender.

Ces rhapsodes qui déambulent
Dès que tombent les crépuscules
Vont chansonnant choses et gens :
Fallièros et sa vaste panse,
Et la façon dont il dépense,
Nouveau Crésus, tous ses argents ;

Ce sont les chansonniers. Leur blague
Transperce comme d'une dague
Les personnages rococos,
Et, débitant la limonade
Qui rend Ioséphiné malade,
Voici le marchand de cocos !

Regarde ces... comment te dire?
Ces éphèbes au doux sourire,
Ayant même allure et même air ;
Regarde-les : c'est un chapitre
De « *Lucien* » ; « *Lucien* », c'est le titre
Du livre de Binet-Valmer.

Puis, après ces éphèbes roses
Ne voyant que l'envers des choses,
Ces dames en péplos d'Elbeuf
Vont embrasser... l'art dramatique
Et s'exercer dans la... mimique
Chez la marquise de Paimbœuf.

Puis les péripatéticiennes,
Laïs des classes plébéiennes !
Regarde-les, rival d'Ajax :
Sur les Boul-Exter cela grouille,
Ça grouille comme la grenouille...
Bré ké ké kex ! Koax ! Koax !

Those singers who stroll along
After the twilight falls
Sing of things and people:
Of Fallièros[48] and his huge belly,
And of the manner he spends,
Like a new Croesus, all his money;[49]

These are the minstrels. Their jokes
Pierce like a dagger
The rococo characters,
Who dislike lemonade
Which makes Iosephine ill,[50]
Here is the seller of cocaine drink![51]

Look at them . . . what shall I tell you?
These punks with sweet smiles,
Having the same allure and the same air;
Look at them: this a chapter
From "*Lucien*"; "*Lucien*," is the title[52]
Of a book by Binet-Valmer.[53]

Then, after the punks with rosy cheeks
See only the seedy side of things,
These women in tunics by Elbeuf[54]
Will espouse . . . the dramatic art
And engage in . . . mimicry
At the home of the Marquess of Paimbœuf.[55]

Then come the streetwalkers,
Laïs, of the lowest class![56]
Look at them, O rival of Ajax:[57]
On the Avenue Exter they bitch and grumble,[58]
Grumble like a frog. . . .[59]
Bré ké ké kex! Koax! Koax![60]

Et derrière ces hétaïres
Marchent leurs propriétaïres,
Cachant leurs mines de fripons
Sous la coiffure emblématique
Que vous appelez en Attique
La casquette à trois Hellesponts.

Evohé ! Ce sont les modèles
De nos actuels Praxitèles
Et de nos modernes Zeuxis,
Régals d'artistes et de princes
Et dont au fond de vos provinces
Rêve le jeune Anacharsis.

And behind these courtesans
Walk their pimps,
Hiding their tricky looks
Under the emblematic headdress
Which you call in Attica[61]
Three Hellenicornered hat.

Evohé! these are the models
Of our current Praxiteles[62]
And of our modern Zeuxis,[63]
Feasts of artists and princes
And there in the depth of your provinces
The young Anacharsis dreams.[64]

Quoi donc, Ulysse, tu frissonnes !
Serait-ce ces jeunes personnes
Qui t'ont mis dans cet état-là ?
Regarde alors cette ingénue,
Qui n'a, pour voiler sa chair nue,
Comme Eve, qu'un serpent boa :

C'est la piquante midinette,
C'est le trottin, la trottinette,
C'est surtout la « petite main »
Qui finira, je le parie,
Pourvu que Dieu lui prête vie,
Duchesse au faubourg Saint-Germain.

De ce regard plein de promesse,
De ce jeune corps de faunesse,
Hein ! que penses-tu, mon gaillard ?
Auprès d'elle, j'ose le dire,
Platon deviendrait un satyre
Et le vieux Lycurgue un paillard !...

Alors?!... Tu restes impassible ?
Mais vois : Eros a pris pour cible
Tes vieux compagnons Ithaquois !
C'est à croire que le perfide
A trempé dans la cantharide
Les flèches d'or de son carquois.

Why then, Ulysses, you shiver!
Was it these young women
Who put you in this state?
Look now at this budding female,
Who has nothing to cover her naked flesh,
Like Eve, except for a boa snake:

It is the smart dressmaker,[65]
It is the streetwalker, male and female,
But above all, it is "the seamstress"
Who will ultimately, I'll bet you,
Alter what God has given life,
The Duchess of Faubourg Saint-Germain.[66]

Of this gaze full of promise,
Of this young body of a female faun,
What do you say! what do you think, my jolly fellow?
In her presence, I dare say,
Plato would become a satyr[67]
And Lycurgus a lecherous old man! . . .[68]

Well?!. . you remain immune?
But look: Eros has marked for a target[69]
Your old Ithacan companions!
The treacherous fellow probably
Dipped into the aphrodisiac
The golden arrows of his quiver.

Vois ! Ils la suivraient jusqu'en Thrace ;
Fais comme eux, marche sur leur trace,
Au galop, Ulysse, au galop !
Et le sage Ulysse de dire,
Moitié larmes, moitié sourire :
« Ah ! les salops ! Ah ! les salops ! »

Look! They have followed her till Thrace;[70]
Do as they do, follow in their footsteps,
Hurry up, Ulysses, hurry up!
And the prudent Ulysses says,
Half in tears and half in smiles:
"Ah! the sluts! Ah! the sluts!"[71]

DEUXIEME TABLEAU

Le faux pas d'Ulysse

———

LE RÉCITANT

Cependant, les compagnons d'Ulysse, avec la hâte fébrile que peuvent donner huit ans de navigation, ont suivi le jeune trottin qui les a conduits directement rue Kabanès, dans une maison mystérieuse où la patronne, faisant preuve du plus large esprit de tolérance, accueille avec une égale affabilité les indigènes et les métèques, pourvu qu'ils soient lestés de mines, de talents et de drachmes.

SECOND TABLEAU

The Faux Pas of Ulysses

THE NARRATOR

Meanwhile, Ulysses's companions, with the feverish haste which eight years of sailing can give, pursue a young camp follower who leads them directly to a mysterious house in rue Kabanès,[72] where the Madam, expressing a most tolerant spirit, receives graciously with equal affability the native and the foreigner, provided they are loaded with hêmina, talents and drachmas.[73]

Nous voici rue Kabanès.

Il est huit heures du soir, heure à laquelle ces dames se préparent aux sacrifices. Elles attendent le coiffeur, qui paraît sous les traits reconnaissables de M. Max Dearly. C'est un homme affairé. Il doit encore aller rue Feydos et rue Monthyon, dans d'autres établissements similaires fréquentés par de joyeux vivants qui, en fait de philosophes, ont surtout compulsé Désaugiers et lu Panard.

Il entraîne ses clientes vers le salon de coiffure, cependant que Madame vient jeter sur le temple le coup d'œil du maître ou plutôt de la sous-maîtresse.

On sonne.

C'est Kouèros, le fameux rasta : Rasta-Kouèros, que l'on a surnommé le procureur général. Il vient proposer à Madame de lui amener cet étranger dont toute la ville s'entretient, ce guerrier enrichi des dépouilles de Troie, qu'il a rencontré à son cercle. Madame, flairant un client sérieux, promet à Kouèros la forte commission.

Deux jeunes élèves du lycée Michelès se sont cotisés pour réunir une somme d'ailleurs infime et s'offrent à vider leur bourse entre les mains de la patronne. Celle-ci déclare la somme insuffisante, mais, émue par tant de jeunesse, elle ne veut pas laisser partir les potaches sans quelque réconfort et, s'offrant elle-même en holocauste, elle court leur prodiguer dans une pièce voisine les secours de son art.

Here we are at rue Kabanès.

It is eight o'clock in the evening, the hour at which these women prepare themselves for sacrifice. They go to the hairdresser, who appears to be influenced by the recognizable styles of Monsieur Max Dearly.[74] This is a busy man. We must still go to rue Feydos[75] and rue Monthyon,[76] where there are similar establishments frequented by those who enjoy happy living and who, following the ideas of some philosophers, have above all examined Désaugiers[77] and read Panard.[78]

He hurries his clients toward the hairdresser shop while Madam glances briefly at the temple with the eye of a boss or rather his female deputy.

There is a ring at the door.

This is Kouèros, the famous adventurer: Rasta-Kouèros,[79] who has been nicknamed Procurer-General. He suggests that Madam accompany this stranger so the whole city will be able to meet him, this warrior enriched by the spoils of Troy, and whom he met on his own turf. Madam, smelling a serious client, promises Kouèros a handsome commission.

Two young students of the Michelès High School [appear].[80] They got together a small sum of money so they can empty their pockets into the hands of the Madam. The Madam tells them that the money is not enough, but, moved by their youth, she does not want to let the youngsters leave without some relief and offers them herself as a substitute sacrifice. She lures them into a nearby room and helps with her skills.

Mais Figaros a terminé sa tâche; grâce à lui, des chichis savants et des postiches prestigieux ont rendu à ces dames toute leur splendeur capillaire. Les clients peuvent venir. Et les clients viennent.

Voici les compagnons d'Ulysse conduits par le pseudo-trottin qui n'était autre qu'une habile rabatteuse, si j'ose employer ici une expression vraiment impropre. Elle pousse le cri traditionnel: « Toutes ces dames au gynécée ! »

Ces dames : Phryné, Chrysis, Glycère et Nubiane !...

Toujours sous l'influence de huit ans de navigation, les compagnons d'Ulysse, dédaignant tout préliminaire, s'élancent comme un seul homme, après une courte invocation à Mercure. Ta zoa trekei : les animaux courent.

Cependant Ulysse a réfléchi qu'il était peu courageux d'abandonner ses compagnons dans ce nouveau danger et, renseigné par Kouèros, il accourt au temple de la rue Kabanès.

(*Sonnerie.*)

Une voix: Un guerrier monte !

Madame accourt.

— Général, dit-elle avec une aisance qui trahit l'ancienne élève de la Légion d'honneur, soyez ici le bienvenu...

But Figaros[81] has concluded his task; thanks to his efforts, some snobbish scholars and some prestigious and affected fellows had these women with the assistance of all their splendid maidenhair. Clients can now come. And clients came.

Here [are] Ulysses's companions led by the fake streetwalker who is, if I dare use a truly improper expression, none other than a skillful tout. She utters the traditional call: "All women to the gyneceum!"[82]

These women were: Phryné,[83] Chrysis,[84] Glycère,[85] and Nubiane!...[86]

Still under the influence of their eight years of sailing, Ulysses's companions, disdaining all preliminaries, rush as a single man, after a short invocation to Mercury.[87] Ta zoa trekei: the animals are on the run.

Meanwhile Ulysses thought that he showed little courage in abandoning his companions in this unexpected danger, and directed by Kouèros, he hastens to the temple on rue Kabanès.

(Bells ring.)

A voice: A warrior is coming up!

Madam rushes in.

—General, she says with an ease which betrays a former student of the school of the Legion of Honor,[88] you are most welcome here . . .

Ulysse s'incline et dit :

— Madame, rentrez vos boniments à la Grèce; je suis un vieux de la vieille et on ne me la fait pas.

— Cependant, général, j'ai des femmes délicieuses.

— Je les connais, ou plutôt je ne veux pas les connaître. Je viens ici chercher mes camarades pour les aider encore une fois à sortir d'une passe fâcheuse : pass, passa, panne ! Quant à toi, Pompéïa, tu dépenserais en vain des paroles pompeuses; mets un bœuf sur ta langue ! Kléïé kiboton, ferme ta boîte !

Pompéïa, un instant surprise par ce langage énergique, se ravise aussitôt et dit :

— Permets, ô valeureux guerrier, que je te présente le plus pur joyau de mon écrin : la jolie Anthelmys, femme légitime d'un riche banquier dont l'hôtel donne sur l'Agora. Nul homme ne peut résister à ses charmes !

Elle appelle :

— Anthelmys ! Anthelmys !

Puis elle se retire discrètement.

Ulysse jette un regard de confiance sur la statue de Minerve, sa divinité protectrice :

Ulysses pulls himself up and says:

—Madam, hold off your nonsense concerning Greece; I am one of the old stalwarts and I am not susceptible to such a thing.

—However, my General, I have delicious women.

—I know them, or rather I don't want to know them. I come here to look for my comrades and to assist them once more to get them out of an awful mess: a mess, a mess, what a mess![89] As for you, Pompéïa,[90] you are wasting your time with pompous words; keep your own counsel! Kléïé kiboton, shut your mouth![91]

Pompéïa, momentarily surprised by this energetic language, is thrilled and says:

—Allow me, valiant warrior, to present to you the purest jewel in my chest: the beautiful Anthelmys, the legitimate wife of a rich banker whose house stands in the Agora.[92] There is no man who can resist her charms!

She calls:

—Anthelmys! Anthelmys![93]

She then retires discreetly.

Ulysses looks confidently at the statue of Minerva, his divine protectoress:

— O Pallas Athènê, dit-il, daigne soutenir ma vertu !

Mais Anthelmys apparaît. Musique ! (*Orgue.*)

Ulysses'est troublé. Anthelmys se rapproche. Ulysse invoque vainement tous les dieux et Jupiter lui-même : sa chair faiblit. Anthelmys lui rappelle que Jupiter était surtout un dieu marcheur et que pour honorer les dames il se transformait souvent en cygne ou en taureau. Elle n'exigera pas de lui un aussi gros sacrifice, mais s'il veut se transformer en pluie d'or, elle promet de ne pas prendre de parapluie.

Ulysse est vaincu.

— Permets, dit-il, que j'aille secouer la poussière du voyage au lavabos voisin où j'ai vu en entrant une réduction minuscule du cheval de Troie. Quand mes cheveux seront lustrés et mon corps oint des parfums que distille Bicharas, Anthelmys, je t'appellerai !...

La défaite d'Ulysse et le malheur de Pénélope sont d'autant plus assurés qu'Anthelmys se sent pour le héros un irrésistible penchant, béguinos.

Heureusement, Minerve veille.

Se rappelant qu'elle disputa jadis à Vénus et à Junon la pomme de la beauté, elle va user d'un stratagème que lui indiqua Armande, blonde enfant de Lesbos, où elle tenait un cabaret à l'enseigne du Hanneton.

Elle descend de son socle, elle s'avance vers Anthelmys et lui dit :

—O Pallas Athena,[94] he says, deign to sustain my virtue!

But Anthelmys appears. Music! (*Organ*).

Ulysses is disturbed. Anthelmys draws near. In vain Ulysses begins invoking the names of all the gods, including Jupiter himself:[95] his flesh grows weak. Anthelmys reminds him that Jupiter was above all a gay old god, who in order to satisfy women, would turn himself into a swan or a bull. She will not require of him as great a sacrifice, but if he will transform himself into golden rain she will promise not to take out an umbrella.

Ulysses is defeated.

—Allow me, he says, to take off the dust of travel by going to the nearby bathroom where I saw, as I was coming in a miniature version of the Trojan horse. When my hair is polished and my body is anointed with perfumes which emit the sweet smell of incense, Anthelmys, I shall call you! . . .

The defeat of Ulysses and the misery of Penelope are now certain as Anthelmys feels for the hero an irresistible attraction and sweet appeal.

Happily, Minerva is watching.

Recalling that she once vied with Venus and Juno[96] for the golden apple to affirm her beauty, she uses the strategy of appearing as Armande,[97] the blond girl of Lesbos,[98] who has a cabaret run in accordance with the teachings of Hanneton.[99]

She comes down from her pedestal, she walks toward Anthelmys and says to her:

Anthelmys, sois rassurée :
Si du ciel olympien
Et de la voûte azurée
Je descends, c'est pour ton bien !

Anthelmys, que vas-tu faire
Avec ce guerrier brutal
Dont l'amour est terre à terre,
Dont le baiser fait du mal ?

D'autant plus qu'il a, j'y pense,
Plus de huit ans de vertu ;
Pour ton rhume, en l'occurrence,
Mignonne, que prendras-tu ?

D'une effroyable avalanche
Tu croiras subir le choc ;
Il va sur ta chair si blanche
Se ruer comme un auroch !

Anthelmys, rest assured:
If by the Olympian heaven
And by the blue yonder
I come down, it is in your interest!

Anthelmys, what are you going to do
With this fierce warrior
Whose love is vulgar,
Whose kiss brings evil?

I think, even more important than that,
Is that he has kept his virtue for eight years;
For such an illness, when it occurs,
Dainty girl, what do you take?

Of such a dreadful avalanche
Do you think you can withstand the shock;
He will on your white body
Throw himself like a bison!

Puis quand il t'aura brisée
Aussitot tu le verras
Dormir sans t'avoir bercée
Un instant entre ses bras,

Et, ronflant tel un Vésuve,
Il sera jusqu'au matin
Comme un ivrogne qui cuve
Le falerne du festin !

Vois-tu ! c'est ainsi qu'est l'homme :
Pour lui, la femme toujours
N'est qu'une bête de somme,
Mais il est d'autres amours !

Je sais une ile de songe,
Ile de bonheur divin
Où le baiser se prolonge,
Où la caresse est sans fin :

Là sur les ruisseaux s'effeuillent
Les neiges de l'amandier,
Là les roses ont des feuilles
D'un charme particulier ;

Des fruits faisant la cueillette
Tu connaîtras les douceurs,
Les douceurs de la dinette
Avec les Nymphes, mes sœurs.

Mais je vois la pointe exquise
De ton sein qui se raidit,
Je te sens déjà conquise !
Mon petit doigt me l'a dit.

Laissons ton guerrier barbare
Tremper dans son lavabos,
Et courons jusqu'à la gare
Prendre le train pour Lesbos !...

Then when you are broken
You will understand quickly
Sleeping without delusions
In one moment in his arms,

And, rumbling like a Vesuvius,[100]
He will stay till morning
Like a drunkard who lets sleep off
The good wine of the banquet!

You see! it is like this for a man:
For him the woman is always
Nothing but an animal to sleep with,
Yet there are other kinds of love!

I know of a dream island,
An island of divine happiness
Where a kiss lingers,
And a caress has no end:

There into the streams falls
The snow from the almond tree,
There the roses have petals
With peculiar charms;

Of the fruits ripening for the harvest
You will recognize the sweetnesses,
The sweetnesses of dining
With the Nymphs, my sisters.[101]

But I see the delicate spot
In your chest which stiffens,
I feel that you're already conquered!
My little finger has told me.

Let your savage warrior
Soak in his bath[102]
And let's run to the railroad station
To catch the train for Lesbos! . . .

ULYSSE (*dans la coulisse*) :
Air: *Izeil.*

Anthelmys, fille peu farouche,
J'ai soif de ton corps sans pareil !
Porte-moi la fleur de ta bouche,
J'ai soif de ton baiser vermeil !...

LE RÉCITANT

Ulysse appelle en vain sa bien-aimée. Ne la voyant pas venir, il s'est habillé à la hâte et il vient la chercher, car il urge! il urge!

O déception! Anthelmys est partie et c'est la majestueuse Pompéïa qui apparaît.

Elle écoutait à la porte, elle a entendu tout le pallas de Minerve et assisté, en mortelle impuissante, à l'enlèvement d'Anthelmys par la déesse. Elle ne regrette d'ailleurs qu'une chose, c'est de ne pas être du voyage.

Mais Ulysse, exacerbé, ne lui laisse pas le temps de réfléchir. Il l'entraîne vers le triclinium voisin, cependant qu'elle murmure, Fà la fois surprise et charmée : « Ma mère ! Ma mère ! »

[Ulysses: *from the wings*]:
A tune: *Izeil*

Anthelmys, my shy little girl,
I am thirsty for your exquisite body!
Bring me the flower of your mouth,
I am thirsty for a rosy kiss! . . .

THE NARRATOR

Ulysses calls his sweet love in vain. When he realizes she is not coming, he hastily dresses and comes out to look for her, for he has the urge! the urge!

O deception! Anthelmys is gone, and it is the majestic Pompéïa who appears.

She has listened behind the door, she has heard all of Minerva's flattery, of the mortal weakness, and witnessed the elevation of Anthelmys by the goddess. She regrets only one thing, that she is not on this voyage.

But an exacerbated Ulysses does not leave himself time to think. He hurries toward the nearest dining hall, while surprised and bewitched she murmurs: "My Mother! My Mother!"

TROISIEME TABLEAU

Le départ d'Ulysse

——

LE RÉCITANT

Or, Ulysse et ses compagnons ont épuisé la coupe des plaisirs montmartrois. On les a vus successivement au Monicos, au Mus-Necus, autrement dit : Rat Mort, à l'abbaye de Thélèmé, au bal Tabarinos, et cæteron, et cæteron...

Pourtant le sage Ulysse s'est ressaisi. Un matin il a fait sonner le ralliement dans des conques marines et donner le signal du départ.

THIRD TABLEAU

The Departure of Ulysses

THE NARRATOR

Well, Ulysses and his companions having exhausted the contents of the chalice of Montmartarian pleasures, roamed successively Monicos,[103] Mus-Necus,[104] otherwise known as: The Dead Rat, Thelemachus's Abbey,[105] Bal Tabarinos,[106] etc., etc. . . .

However the prudent Ulysses finally got hold of himself. One morning he rang the assembly call for his seaworthy sailors and gave the order for departure.

Et voici les vainqueurs d'Ilion. Ah ! ce ne sont plus ces émules d'Akilleus, ces Grecs au pied léger, podas okus. Ils évoquent plutôt un tableau célèbre : les Dernières cartouches. Tirant l'aine et traînant le pied, ils vont procéder à l'appareillage. Bientôt les trirèmes, comme de grands oiseaux, déploient au loin leurs ailes fauves. Le fils de Laërte repart pour de nouvelles aventures.

Sur le rivage, ne pouvant se consoler du départ d'Ulysse et de ses compagnons, la majestueuse Pompéïa et ses compagnes viennent verser des pleurs. Un embonpoint significatif nous révèle que ces messieurs leur ont laissé quelques souvenirs de leur passage...

LE CHŒUR :

Air : *La Mer*, d'Adolf Stanislas.

Yo ! Yo ! Yo !
Adieu, rive si belle
Où Pallas immortelle
Conduisit nos vaisseaux !
Vers la rive propice
Que ta trirème glisse ! . .
Puisses-tu, sage Ulysse,
Voir la fin de tes maux !

Et les enfants issus de ce commerce perpetuèrent jusqu'à nous les traditions d'art, de littérature et d'amour, juste orgueil de la Grèce antique et du Montmartre actuel... et le onzième arrière-petit-fils du prudent Ulysse n'était autre, vous n'en serez pas surpris, Mesdames et Mes-sieurs, que le onzième arrière-grand-père de M. Maurice Donnay, du Chat français et de l'Académie noire.

Here are the conquerors of Troy. Ah, they are no longer a worthy match of Achilles,[107] these Greeks with a nimble foot, podas okus. They evoke rather a famous painting: *The Last Bullets*.[108] Pulling the groin and dragging the foot, they proceed to their vessels. Soon the triremes, like great birds, deploy in the distance their tawny wings. And the son of Laertes[109] is on his way to new adventures. . .

On the banks of the river, the majestic Pompéïa and her retinue, unable to reconcile themselves to the departure of Ulysses and his companions, shed tears. The women's round bellies reveal that these gentlemen left many souvenirs of their passing through.

THE CHORUS:

After the tune: *La Mer*, by Adolf Stanislas

Yo! Yo! Yo!
Farewell, beautiful banks
Where the immortal Pallas
Guides your vessels!
Toward the propitious bank
That the trireme glides! . . .
May you, prudent Ulysses,
See the end of all your troubles!

And so the offspring of this venture until our present time continue the traditions of arts, of literature and of love, the rightful pride of ancient Greece and of the contemporary Montmartre . . . and the eleventh great grandson of the prudent Ulysses is none other, you are not going to be surprised, ladies and gentlemen, than the eleventh great grandson of Monsieur Maurice Donnay[110] the offspring of the French Cat[111] and the Black Academy.[112]

Notes to the Text

1. Paul Escudier: A contemporary journalist who wrote feature articles in various newspapers.

2. Ulysses: The Latin name for Odysseus. The protagonist of Homer's *Odyssey*, known for his cunning. He wandered for years on his return from the Trojan War to his home in Ithaca while his wife Penelope remained faithful fending off suitors and weaving her tapestry.

3. Naiades: Water nymphs. The Naiades were the subject of one of the poems in Pierre Louÿs's *Les Chansons de Bilitis* (*The Songs of Bilitis*).

4. Cyclades: A collection of Islands in the Aegean, mentioned by Pierre Louÿs.

5. Sirens: Birds with women's heads found in the *Odyssey*, they preyed on mariners.

6. Nausicaa: Daughter of Alcinous, the Phaeacian king. In the *Odyssey* she received Ulysses in the course of his wandering and treated him kindly.

7. Cahen-caha: The phrase "as they say in the synagogue" is misleading, perhaps deliberately so. It is a transliteration of Hebrew words meaning "diminished priest" or "unworthy priest" and may be a reference to the chastity imputed to Ulysses in the play. In the wake of the Dreyfus affair, just the mention of synagogue may have carried other connotations. In French the phrase is usually written "cahin-caha," a corruption of the

Latin *qua hinc, qua hic,* "both here and there" (i.e., "neither here nor there"), and its use in French goes back as far as the fifteenth century. See *Littré*, 435. When pronounced by a Frenchman, *Cahen* or *Cahin* sounds much like "Cain," a minor poet who, in 1907, lost a duel with the publisher of *Le Matin* and whose name came to mean "a loser." Many of those who visited La Lune Rousse would have known the story and so would have picked up the reference. See also the note to Panard, below. There is one more reference to Cahin-caha in the popular song by Léon Xanrof (1867-1953) entitled *Le Fiacre* (1890) which goes:

> Une Fiacre allait trottinant,
> Cahin Caha
> Hu' dia! Hop là!

See Harold B. Seigel, *Turn-of-the-Century Cabaret,* 46. *Cahin-caha* was the constant theme of the song to indicate along with *Hu' dia! Hop là*, the sound of trotting. Ulysses was leaving as he was trotting, "En s'en allant Cahen-caha."

8. Circe: Kirké, daughter of Helios, known for her magic powers. When Ulysses and his men landed on her island, she gave his men drinks which turned them into pigs but later changed them back to men. Ulysses and his companions enjoyed her "hospitality" for many years before their return to Ithaca.

9. Penelope: Ulysses's faithful wife.

10. Pindar: The great poet of ancient Greece (522-442 B.C.).

11. Calmann-Lévy: Well-known French publishing firm. Gustave Calmann had significant influence in the world of literature during the first decades of the twentieth century.

12. Galen: Galen (Gallenos) 129-199 A.D. An influential medical scientist and physician in the Hellenic age. His writings were preserved by the Arabs and translated during the Renaissance. The attribution of the invention of the chastity belt to Galen is erroneous. The earliest mention of this device was in Homer's *Odyssey,* when the god Hephaestos forged a chastity net to put an end to the infidelities of his wife, Venus, during his absence.

13. Venus: Aphrodite. Greek goddess of love.

14. Jupe: For Jupiter. Old Jupe is a liberal translation for *vieux Jupin. Jupin* also means little skirt.

15. Ilion: The City of Troy. The reference here is to the railroad line: Paris-Lyon-Marseilles.

16. Icarus: The son of Daedalus, the legendary inventor, engineer and craftsman. He participated in his father's experiment to build wings

and fly to safety, but he flew too close to the sun, which melted the wax that held on his wings, and fell into the sea and drowned. Flying, a new and dangerous sport at the time, was increasing in Europe and the United States in 1910. In January 1910 the French aviator Paulhan flew in California at the then-high altitude of 1524 meters: the previous record was 1000 meters. Paulhan was challenged by the Russian aviator Efimov in Verona, Italy. Although he did not break his previous record, he nevertheless won first prize. Chavez, who flew over the Alps in September 1910 crashed at Domodossola and smashed his legs and died a few days later. Earlier, in August 1908, the Wright Brothers flew their machine at Le Mans.

17. Daedalus: Legendary inventor. His name means "master craftsman." According to myth he built the labyrinth in Crete for King Minos to house the minotaur, to which he was subsequently confined by Minos with his son Icarus. He escaped captivity by making wings for himself and his son that transported them off the island.

18. Eukrêtinos: In Greek this word means ignorant. In the French it is a compound of the *eu* as in Eucharist and *crétin*, stupid.

19. Beta: The second letter of the Greek alphabet; in the French means "stupid, block-headed." *Alpha* and *Omega* mean the "beginning" and the "end."

20. Crouzeix: Creuse is the region where the best French steel originates; at the end of 19th and 20th centuries it was the name of the major steel company in France (see Zola's *Germinal*). The name also suggests Creusa (*Créuse*), the daughter of Priam, King of Troy, and his wife Hecuba. Also Creuse is the mother of Ion, her long lost son, whose name was given to Ionia.

21. Reboux: Possibly a modification of the name of a French establishment. It may be also a reference to Paul Reboux, a contemporary gossip columnist.

22. Vioros: Julien Viaud is the real name of Pierre Loti (1850-1923), a contemporary man of letters. It may also be a reference to Louis François Veuillot (1813-1880), a well-known right wing journalist who preached morality with vehemence. However, the context suggests allusion to an establishment.

23. Bilitis: This is a clear allusion to Pierre Louÿs's famous collection of erotic poems, *Chansons de Bilitis* (1894). The title was changed, by turning one letter upside down to read *Chaussons de Bilitis*. The life of the poetess Bilitis was narrated by Louÿs in the introduction to this collection of fictitious poems, which he wrote in Constantinople in 1894, in which he evoked the names of Tanagra and Praxiteles. Pierre Louÿs (1870-1925) was known for his theory that poetry was brought to the West by the Greeks from the Ionia region.

24. Poulbos: A play on the name of Francisque Poulbot (1879-1946), a contemporary humorous caricaturist who drew the streets of Paris and Montmartre. *Poule*, chick, means prostitute in argot.

25. Corinthian lamps: During La Belle Époque it became fashionable for industrial designers to design table lamps after the bodies of famous dancers. The most memorable is from 1900, by Raoul Larche, modeled after Loïe Fuller.

26. Priam: King of Troy.

27. Galicos: Possibly a reference to the *galli*, who were the eunuchs of Cybele, the goddess of fertility. They are also considered disinterested parties in the art of go-between.

28. Galleries Pygmalion: Pygmalion's name was used to suggest a reference to the newly fashionable department stores in Paris.

29. Thucydides: The name of the Greek historian Thucydides (460-400 B.C.) is given to a department store.

30. Cent-Kiloï: This double pun means clearly the woman who weighs a hundred kilograms (220 pounds), but also suggests *sans culottes*, "without pants."

31. Diana: Goddess associated with Artemis, the moon-goddess. She is known by her cult followers as *trivia* for being worshiped on the roads.

32. Bobinos: Derived from the name of the brothel Bobino.

33. Egine: The name of an island in Greece and possibly an allusion to *egide*, "protector" (a pimp) in the opera *Louise* (1900) about the life of a seamstress in Montmartre by Gustave Charpentier (1860-1956): *"there were glamour girls and their protectors."*

34. Tanagra: A Greek city which became famous in modern times for the discovery of terracotta statuettes. It was mentioned in Louÿs's *Les Chansons de Bilitis.*

35. Agathos and Agatha: *Agathon*, a joint pseudonym, after the Greek tragic poet (mentioned in *The Frogs* by Aristophanes) of two conservative literary critics who early in the twentieth century wrote and published together: Henri Massis and Alfred de Tarde. This must have been an inside joke.

36. Hippo taxi: A horse drawn cab.

37. Eyrénès Fulakoï: The keeper of the peace, or the chief of police who, in this case, marches in front of bands on festive occasions.

38. Sergoï: Possible nickname for the police chief.

39. "Little girl from Brittany"; "He has no Umbrella"; "Come on Poupoule": Titles of popular songs. The Greek is loosely rendered.

40. Tyrtée: Tyrtaeus, a Spartan poet from the 7th century B.C.

41. Yon-Lugas: Yon-Lug, born Constant Jaquet in 1864, studied

architecture in Lyon. Slightly hunchbacked, he joined a traveling animal act, and later a theatre company in Lyon: *Théâtre des Ombres Lyriques*. He took up the name Yon Lug and became a chansonier and headed toward Montmartre. He worked often with Bonnaud yet remained a wandering minstrel. He thought of himself as an artist in the tradition of Molière, who died during one of his performances. He predicted his own ending to be same. It happened that way in 1921.

42. Hotel of "Reunited Voyagers": a modification of the name of one of the cafés in Montmartre: *Rendez-vous des Mariniers*.

43. Neptune: An Italian god with the same attributes as Poseidon. According to Homer, it was Poseidon who interfered with the prompt and safe return of Ulysses to Ithaca.

44. Montmartre: The 18th district of Paris known for its cabarets and artistic studios. It is believed that its name was derived from the hill where the martyrdom of Saint Denis and his companions took place.

45. Mountjoy: In the context of the text uttered in the play it means the Hill of Joy, yet it is also an allusion to a medieval line from the epic *Chanson de Roland*. The name of Saint Denis, which relates Montmartre to Montjoie, evokes the memory of the bishop, who was sent around 250 A.D. to preach to the people of Paris against sin and who was martyred on the hill.

46. Hill of Love: An allusion to the female pubic area, The Mount of Venus.

47. Minerva: An Italian goddess often identified with Athena.

48. Fallièros: An important person, after the President of France Armand Faillièrs, who served from 1906-1913.

49. Croesus: The name of the last king of Lydia. He is connected with the ability to make good judgment and enormous wealth.

50. Lemonade which makes Iosephine ill: a "Josephine" was a blonde owner of "Sherry-Cobbler," a small brasserie at Boulevard St. Michel. Her origins were unknown and after she disappeared she became a cult figure. As legend had it, she was last seen as a saloonkeeper in Texas. The other "Josephine" was the Empress of France who was lampooned in Caran d'Ache's *Epopée*, performed earlier as a piece of Ombres Chinoises at the Chat Noir Cabaret.

51. Coco (Licorice Drink): There are two meanings for the word coco in argot: *coco*, a licorice drink sold on the streets; also it means "cocaine." The context indicates that the former is used to allude to the latter. It is also a a nonsensical rhyme with rococo.

52. Lucien: The title of a novel by Gustave Binet-Valmer. The name also alludes to Lucian, the Hellenestic philosopher and satirist (115-200 A.D.), who in *Dialogues of the Courtesans*, satirized the practices of

lesbians. See Harold Greenwald & Aron Krich (Ed.), *The Prostitute in Literature*, 42. There are three Luciens in the performing group of the play: Lucien Boyer, also one of the authors; Victor Tourtal whose original name was Lucien; and Miss Lucy Pezet.

53. Binet-Valmer: Gustave Binet-Valmer (1875-1940), writer and commentator on the arts known for his severe judgments and brutal treatment of innovative activities.

54. Elboeuf: A town in France where there was a factory which manufactured garments.

55. Paimboeuf: A clear allusion to Colette's friend Marquess Belboeuf, who wrote a Sapphic scenario for her writer friend, who danced to it semi-naked. It is also a reference to a well-known fat Baroness nicknamed *La Brioche*, who kept a young poetess as a lover. Since *pain* means "bread" in French, it may be another reference to the fat Baroness, who appeared earlier as the fat lady who weighs one-hundred kilos.

56. Laïs: The name of one of two famous Greek courtesans.

57. Ajax: The brave hero of the Greeks in the war against Troy. He competed with Ulysses for Achilles's shield.

58. Avenue Exter: A name of a street which since 1910 is not recognizable. However, Exter is composed of *ex* and *ter*, "out of this world."

59. Frogs: They appeared in *The Frogs* by Aristophanes.

60. *Bré ké ké kex ! Koax Koax*: A line spoken repeatedly by the chorus of frogs in Hades in Aristophanes's play. (Aristophanes often opposed and ridiculed male and female homosexuality.)

61. Attica: The southern region of Greece where Athens is its largest city.

62. Praxiteles: The great sculptor of ancient Greece from the 4th century A.D. who is known for his *Aphrodite of Knedos*.

63. Zeuxis: A Greek painter from the 5th century B.C. who was responsible for what became known as the School of Athens.

64. Anacharsis: A Scythian king (circa 600 B.C.) known for his intelligence. He is responsible for instituting the festival of Athens, which gathered artists and performers, after visiting, during his extensive travels, a festival which honored the goddess Cybele. Lucian attributed to him the invention of the potter's wheel.

65. Midinette: The name of the assistant dressmakers, who strolled Paris streets during their lunch hour (*midi*nettes).

66. Faubourg Saint-Germain: The street in Paris where the upper classes lived; often mentioned in gossip columns, and later by Proust.

67. Plato: (472-348 A.D.) The Greek philosopher, author of *The Republic*.

68. Lycurgus: The great king of Edones in Thrace. He is recognized for ordering the preservation of the Greek tragedies.

69. Eros: The Greek god of love, son of Aphrodite (Venus).

70. Thrace: Tthraki, a region north of Macedonia near the Black Sea.

71. Salops: Sluts, the word is a homophone which sounds like *salauds*, "filthy."

72. Rue Kabanès: At the time Rue Chabanais, a red-light district known for its famous whorehouses.

73. Hêmina: A large unit; drachma: a small unit of Greek currency.

74. Max Dearly: The stage name of Max Rolland. Dearly was a popular comedy actor on the French stage at the turn of the century. He appeared in affected roles and played an English dandy as a result of his early work in music halls. He was skillful in dance and pantomime and a very inventive stage actor. See Beatrix Dussane, *Dieux des Planches*, 138-149.

75. Rue Feydos: The mention of Rue Feydeau, which existed in Paris since the 18th century, is an allusion to the popular author of racy farces, Georges Feydeau (1862-1921), and his father, a novelist who contributed to the realist movement, Ernest Feydeau (1821-1872).

76. Rue Monthyon: Rue de Montyon was a street in Montmartre named after a philanthropist, Jean-Baptiste-Antoine de Montyon (1733-1820), who donated large sums of money for prizes to be given to works which affirmed high moral values.

77. Désaugiers: Marc-Antoine Désaugiers (1772-1827), chansonier.

78. Panard: Charles François Panard (1674-1764), chansonier. In one of his songs there is a line "La vertu va Cahin Caha." See footnote 7 for "Cahin-caha."

79. Rasta-Kouèros: A transposition of the word *rastaqouère*, "vagrant," taken from the Latin American Spanish *rastacuero*, "he who lives without visible means of support."

80. Lycée Michelès: There was no lycée in Paris with such a name. This an allusion to the famous Lycée Montaigne, named after Michel de Montaigne (1533-1592), the great French essayist.

81. Figaros: A reference to the early mentioned hairdresser. The word *figaro* means barber; Figaro was the leading character in Beaumarchais's plays. It is possible that the word is used in the plural to refer to the moralist columnists of *Le Figaro*. It is also a possible allusion to Baron Barbier (Barber), a sometime poet and a technical director at Le Chat Noir.

82. Gyneceum: Probably the place where whores were sent periodically for a medical examination.

83. *Phryné*: The title of a shadow play by Maurice Donnay produced at Le Chat Noir, performed in 1891, and the name of its leading character.

84. Chrysis: The name of the heroine of *Aphrodite: moeurs antiques* (1896), an erotic novel by Pierre Louÿs (1870-1925). Chrisis was an Alexandrian courtesan of Syrian origin.

85. Glycére: A character in Pierre Louÿs's *Aphrodite*.

86. Nubiane: A derivation from the word *Nubienne*, the best-known house of prostitution in Rue Chabanais advertised as having girls from all nationalities. According to *The Pretty Women of Paris, Being a complete Directory or guide for Pleasures for Visitors to the Gay City in 1880's or 1890's*, this house had "the first bagno in the world." Each room was decorated in a different style, regardless of expense. The bathing chamber was sumptuously arranged and could be used in the company of a chosen nymph for the charge of 100 francs. The management issued an illustrated book giving a view of the principal salons. A negress was available in the establishment. This was a favorite resort of upper-class men, and many ladies both in society and out of it came here alone, or with their lovers, for lesbian diversions. See Ian Littlewood, *Paris: A Literary Companion*, 57. The word means "black woman," the name given to a black fashion and artistic model. Nubienne had a long history in the interior decoration of cafés in Montmartre, following in 1838 Charles Gleyre (1818-1874), an "Orientalist" painter, who painted *La Nubienne* as decoration in Montmartre, "a life-size figure of fantasy." See Hugh Honour, *The Image of the Black in Western Art*, 67.

87. Mercury: The Roman god of alacrity, identified with Hermes, the messenger of the gods.

88. Legion of Honor: Dominique Bonnaud's father was a clerk in the Administration of the Legion d'Honneur. In 1804 Napoleon established a number of educational institutions called *Maisons d'Éducation de la Légion d'Honneur* for the instruction of girls who were daughters of members of the order of the Legion of Honor. The schools taught manners, deportment, and home economics.

89. Passe: The verb means to move on, go through; as a noun it also means a house of prostitution. *Pass, passe* are nonsensical utterances made by a magician while performing a card trick. *Panne*: In argot it means "stuck, left in a lurch." *Pass, passe, panne* means going, going, gone.

90. Pompéïa: The character is probably fashioned after Madam Kelly, the famous madam of 12 Rue Chabanais. The name is a direct

allusion to the city of Pompeii. See footnote 100 for Vesuvius. It is also possible that such a name corresponds with pimp[éïa].

91. Kléïé kiboton: A Greek expression, "shut up," or "Shut your box."

92. Agora: The reference to the rich banker in the marketplace the Agora; the husband of Anthelmys. "Agora" is related to the "Song of the Happy Husband" in Louÿs's *Les Chansons de Bilitis*, whose name was Agorakites.

93. Anthelmys: *Anthelminthique* is the scientific name of a poison which is more effective on cold-blooded creatures.

94. Pallas: A title of reverence connected with Athena/Minerva. However, it suggests a double entendre, for *palas* in the French argot also means farter.

95. Jupiter: The supreme god of Rome, identified with the Greek god Zeus.

96. Juno: The supreme goddess of Rome, identified with Hera, the wife of Zeus.

97. Armande: The name of the owner of Le Hanneton, a café frequented by lesbians.

98. Lesbos: An island of considerable size off the coast of Asia Minor where Sappho, a poetess, and her followers took residence.

99. Haneton: Le Hanneton was a café located in Rue Pigalle in Montmartre known for its lesbian clienteles. Among them were Colette and her friend the Marquess Belbeuf.

100. Vesuvius: The volcano near Naples. It erupted in 79 A.D. and destroyed the town of Pompeii with its inhabitants. In the 19th century there was a belief among moralist authors that the town was destroyed by Vesuvius, who represented the wrath of God, because of its decadence and immoral indulgence. Archeological discoveries indicated a high level of sexual freedom in Pompeii at the time of its destruction. Vesuvius erupted once more in April 1906.

101. This scene provides many recollections of Lucian's *Dialogues*.

102. Taking a bath in a brothel was a novel fashion at the time. See footnote 86 for Nubiane.

103. Monicos: Café Monico in Montmartre.

104. Mus-Necus: *Le Rat Mort* (The Dead Rat), a café in Montmartre.

105. Thelemachus Abbey: L'Abbaye de Thélème, a café in Montmartre named after Ulysses's son.

106. Bal Tabarinos: Bal Tabarin, a café in Montmartre.

107. Achilles: The hero of the Greeks during the Trojan War and Ulysses's competitor.

108. *The Last Bullets* (*Les Dernières Cartouches*): A painting by Alphonse Marie de Neuville (1836-1885) whose specialty was painting military subjects.

109. Laertes: The name of Ulysses's father.

110. Maurice Donnay: A French dramatist (1859-1945) educated as a civil engineer. His literary beginnings were at Chat Noir in 1891 with *Phyrné*. After achieving popularity as a playwright he was elected to the French Academy in 1907.

111. French Academy: L'Academie Française, established by Richelieu in 1634.

112. Black Cat: Le Chat Noir, the famous cabaret in Montmartre, founded by Rodolphe Salis (1852-1897) in 1881.

Biographies

DOMINIQUE BONNAUD: Born in Paris 1864, the son of the head of the Grande Chancellerie de la Légion d'honneur. He was a poor student at the Lycée Orléans, but earned his high school diploma at Lycée Charlemagne. In 1895 he worked with Rodolphe Salis at the Chat Noir. He had met Salis earlier in 189 and performed some of his songs intermittently at his Cabaret. He was known for his eloquence and distinct delivery. Founder and co-owner of La Lune Rousse in 1904, and the most famous of the three collaborators who wrote *Ulysse à Montmartre*, he was awarded the Legion of Honor. He died in 1943. La Lune Rousse remained in business at Rue Pigalle until 1964.

NUMA BLÈS: Born Charles Bessat. He was brought up from Marseilles by Dominique Bonnaud. In 1902 he toured the world with Lucien Boyer. Both penniless, they earned their living singing. In Montreal, Canada he was arrested for singing on Sunday during the hours reserved for religious activities. He returned to Paris in 1904. While in Marseilles he had managed a cabaret named La Lune Rousse. In 1904 when he joined Dominique Bonnaud to start a new cabaret, they revived the name: Le Logiz de la Lune Rousse. He died mad as a victim of absinthe in 1918.

LUCIEN BOYER: Born in 1876. He worked as a writer and traveling salesman, dish washer and waiter before he joined Blès and Bonnaud. After his trip around the world with Blès, he joined La Lune Rousse in 1904 as writer, director, performer, and co-owner. He entertained the troops from 1914-1918. In 1922 he received the Legion of Honor as a result of an error, although many thought he nevertheless deserved it. Clemenceau attributed one of his own favorite songs to Boyer. He died in 1942.

YON LUG: Born Constant Jaquet in 1864. He studied architecture in Lyon, then joined a traveling animal act and later a theatre company in Lyon: Théatre des Ombres Lyriques. He then took up the name Yon Lug and became a chansonier and headed for Montmartre. He worked often with Bonnaud yet remained a wandering minstrel. He thought of himself as an artist in the tradition of Molière, who died during one of his performances. He predicted his own ending would be the same. It happened that way in 1921.

GEORGES BALTHA: Born Joseph Glaser-Balthasar in 1873. One of the partners at La Lune Rousse, he worked at the Chat Noir and subsequently at La Morgue Literaire and Quat'z'Arts, always closely associated with Bonnaud's projects. He died in 1939.

PAUL VEIL: Born Paul Briand in Paris in 1865. He was the manager of La Chaumière, a cabaret in Montmartre, and a well-known poet and chansonier. He sang at most of the cabarets in Montmartre. He took a courageous pro-Dreyfus position. In 1914 he founded Le Cabaret de la Chaumière with Victor Tourtal, who died shortly afterwards. Weil received the Legion of Honor in 1938 and died in 1939.

VICTOR TOURTAL: Born Lucien Tourtal. He was nearly beaten to death by a right-wing mob for ridiculing La Contesse de Martel, an outspoken anti-semite. He founded Le Cabaret de la Chaumière with Paul Weil.

LUCY PEZET: One of the original perfomers at Le Cabaret des Quat'z'Arts. She became very popular.

BONDENAT: A veteran designer from the old days of Laplace's Le Cabaret de la Grande Pinte.